The Journey of Community Change

The Journey of Community Change

A How-to Guide for
Healthy Communities·Healthy Youth Initiatives

Jennifer Griffin-Wiesner

A Search Institute Publication

The Journey of Community Change
A How-to Guide for Healthy Communities • Healthy Youth Initiatives

Jennifer Griffin-Wiesner
Copyright © 2005 by Search Institute

A Search Institute Publication

At the time of publication, all facts and figures cited herein are the most current available; all telephone numbers, addresses, and Web site URLs are accurate and active; all publications, organizations, Web sites, and other resources exist as described in this book; and all efforts have been made to verify them. The author and Search Institute make no warranty or guarantee concerning the information and materials given out by organizations or content found at Web sites that are cited herein, and we are not responsible for any changes that occur after this book's publication. If you find an error or believe that a resource listed herein is not as described, please contact Client Services at Search Institute.

10 9 8 7 6 5 4 3
Printed on acid-free paper in the United States of America.

Search Institute
615 First Avenue Northeast, Suite 125
Minneapolis, MN 55413
www.search-institute.org
612-376-8955 • 800-888-7828

ISBN: 1-57482-861-4

Credits
Editors: Kay Hong, Tenessa Gemelke
Book Design: Judy Gilats
Production Coordinator: Mary Ellen Buscher

Library of Congress Cataloging-in-Publication Data
Griffin-Wiesner, Jennifer.
  The journey of community change : a how-to guide for healthy communities • healthy youth initiatives / Jennifer Griffin-Wiesner.
    p. cm.
  Includes bibliographical references.
  ISBN 1-57482-861-4 (pbk. : alk. paper)
  1. Social work with youth. 2. Youth workers. I. Title.

HV1421.G75 2005
362.7'083—dc22
                    2004021681

About Search Institute
Search Institute is an independent, nonprofit, nonsectarian organization whose mission is to provide leadership, knowledge, and resources to promote healthy children, youth, and communities. The institute collaborates with others to promote long-term organizational and cultural change that supports its mission. For a free information packet, call 800-888-7828.

About This Resource
Major support for Search Institute's Healthy Communities • Healthy Youth (HC • HY) initiative was provided by Thrivent Financial for Lutherans. Lutheran Brotherhood, now Thrivent Financial for Lutherans, is the founding national sponsor for HC • HY.

Licensing and Copyright

Printing Tips
To produce high-quality copies of activity sheets for distribution without spending a lot of money, follow these tips:
- Always copy from the original. Copying from a copy lowers the reproduction quality.
- Make copies more appealing by using brightly colored paper or even colored ink. Quick-print shops often run daily specials on certain colors of ink.
- For variety, consider printing each activity sheet on a different color of paper.
- If you are using more than one activity sheet or an activity sheet that runs more than one page, make two-sided copies.
- Make sure the paper weight is heavy enough (use at least 60-pound offset paper) so that the words don't bleed through (as often happens with 20-pound paper).

In memory of Laura Lee Geraghty

Contents

List of Handouts and Worksheets

Chapter 3: Culture and Customs

Chapter 4: Documenting the Journey

Preface

In the midst of my work on this guide to creating an asset-building initiative, my husband and I began planning a trip to New Orleans. It was to be our first time in the Big Easy and we wanted to do it right. Friends and family gave us plenty of conflicting advice: "I loved the French Quarter," said one. "Don't stay in the French Quarter," urged another. "You have to see Bourbon Street at least once; Bourbon Street is overrated, don't bother." "Definitely eat a muffaletta; no, stick with seafood." And so on. I realized one day as we were surfing the Web for ideas that all we really needed was the right book. Initially I had rationalized that because it was only a four-day trip and because we knew so many people who'd been there, we could just wing it. But the truth was that the short time frame and the wealth of possibilities made it even more important to understand the essence of the city and the choices it offered, letting us weave that information with our own interests and intuition.

The guide we chose offered lots of alternatives suited to a variety of travel styles, a quality that helped us adjust our plans when my husband came down with a raging sinus infection on the day of our departure. Fortunately, it also included important context about the culture and customs of this city that often feels like another world. That information came in handy when we found ourselves in the middle of a blocks-long, traffic-stopping, sense-intoxicating jazz funeral procession.

I found, as usual, that despite my acute awareness of being a foreigner, I loved the new tastes, the different smells and sounds, and being myself but somehow altered by the change in context.

Though it never fails to push me beyond my comfort zone, traveling always brings me joy. Perhaps because of this passion, I also find myself frequently defining changes in my life as journeys. Books—memoirs, guided meditations, daily reflections, and so on—are again my faithful and favorite companions, helping me sort through issues, establish priorities, make plans, and take action when appropriate.

These cherished friends provided the inspiration for *The Journey of Community Change*. I have learned, through a lifetime of personal and professional involvement in community change explorations (with more than a decade of that focused on children and youth), that leaders in these efforts need tools that are reliable, accessible, and sensitive to the reality that human endeavors are inevitably unpredictable. The surprises encountered pose challenges, but also make this work beautiful and exciting. You don't need to be told precisely where to go, how to get there, or what to do when you arrive. Instead, I offer an array of options and opinions, information that you can layer with your own experience and expertise. You probably won't carry *The Journey of Community Change* in your backpack, but perhaps you'll keep it on your shelf, turning to it when you need ideas, inspiration, or to adjust your agenda and expectations.

This resource is based on the Developmental Assets framework, which I explain in more detail in the introduction. For now I'll just say that if you choose to take the asset-building road, you have a remarkable adventure ahead of you. Regardless of your current commitment to children and youth, asset building pulls you toward new and delightful ways of thinking, feeling, being, and believing about young people, your community, and yourself.

I hope that sharing the insights of many who have been on the road awhile helps you discover the vision, power, and joy that unites us in this exploration of a healthier, happier way to live.

Jennifer Griffin-Wiesner

Acknowledgments

This book is in your hands because so many people believed in it, and in asset building, and in the power of people to make a positive difference in their communities and in the world. Thanks in particular to asset-building trainers Sue Allen, I. Shelby Andress, Cindy Carlson, Sandra Harris, Keith Pattinson, Marilyn Peplau, and Flora Sánchez; Search Institute President and visionary leader Peter Benson; Jolene Roehlkepartain, author of the original Healthy Communities • Healthy Youth toolkit, upon which *The Journey of Community Change* is based; Search Institute staff members Mary Ackerman, Randi Griner, Kristin Johnstad, Kristie Probst, Gene Roehlkepartain, Patricia Seppanen, Nancy Tellett-Royce, and Lynette Ward, who are working every day to support, teach, and learn from asset champions; the many brave asset champions who often must blaze trails without the benefit of a Global Positioning System; and, finally, to my editors: Kay Hong, who in addition to providing key conceptual and structural guidance, believed in this leg of the journey and in my ability to do it justice in words, and Tenessa Gemelke and Ruth Taswell, who "brought it home."

The Journey
Is the Reward

Welcome aboard! By simply picking up this practical, easy-to-use guidebook, you have taken the first steps on a lifelong journey toward a healthier, more vibrant, youth-friendly community—regardless of where you live. You'll discover through the stories and examples presented here that people across the world in wide-open spaces, bustling cities, and everywhere in between are using the ideas found here to move forward with positive visions for the future.

In Alberta, Canada, for example, the Mounties (Royal Canadian Mounted Police) are issuing tickets for good behavior. In Oklahoma City, fewer teens are becoming parents; other risk behavior rates are also down thanks to an initiative that works to help people in the community make important connections in order to better serve young people. And in Warren County, Pennsylvania, youth and adults are collaborating to create public works of art.

These are tiny glimpses of the big picture of what's known as Search Institute's Healthy Communities • Healthy Youth (HC • HY) initiative. It's an international movement of committed individuals and groups that want to make a difference for *all* people, particularly children and youth.

The trail to HC • HY was blazed in the late 1980s when Search Institute developed and released a new survey designed to help adults better understand adolescents. This research tool asked young people in grades 6 through 12 more than 250 questions about their friends, family, schools, communities, behavioral choices, and beliefs.

In addition to yielding important information about young people's lives, the survey findings sparked an unanticipated result: hundreds of communities and countless individuals were inspired to embark upon intentional and focused efforts to make change happen. Once they recognized the way things were, they wanted to make them better. It is fair to say that for those whose lives have been touched, "home" will never be the same.

Inspiring these journeys were the data that emerged from the studies. They showed clearly that young people were lacking many of the resources, supports, and inner strengths that help them survive and thrive. More startling and groundbreaking was that the young people who did experience these developmental strengths were much better off than their peers: they were more likely to report being involved in leadership, doing well in school, demonstrating positive social behaviors, and taking good care of themselves. The astounding implications ranged from personal (for young people and their families) to social (for schools, health care, law enforcement, juvenile justice, and other systems) to economic (for government agencies, community programs, funders, and others).

Based on this important information about how young people survive and thrive, Search Institute President Peter Benson wrote a report called *The Troubled Journey: A Portrait of 6th–12th Grade Youth*. It presented the evidence and cast a vision for creating healthy, strong communities by engaging adults to help young people experience stronger webs of support, empowerment, boundaries and expectations, constructive use of time, commitment to learning, positive values, social competencies, and positive identity. Benson called these eight areas of strengths *the framework of Developmental Assets* (see the complete list on page 3). The handout "The Power of Assets" (on page 4) shows examples of the power of the assets and why it's so important to strengthen this foundation for our young people.

The power of the assets quickly became evident to a number of forward-thinking community leaders in St. Louis Park, Minnesota. They began talking about and experimenting with the idea of collectively focusing on the positive things that all young people need to succeed in life. They believed that with the right information, ordinary citizens could be empowered to have an extraordinary impact on children and youth in the communities where they live, work, and play. The Developmental Assets framework quickly became a catalyst for mobilizing citizen engagement and action as concerned people from all walks of life realized new ways to work together on behalf of young people. In the process they found that the benefits extended beyond young people. For example:

► Many parents felt affirmed for things they were already doing, and discovered alternatives to frustrating, negative approaches to problem solving.

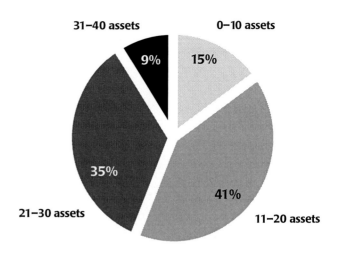

The Gap in Assets among Youth

While there is no "magic number" of assets young people should have, our data indicate that 31 is a worthy, though challenging, benchmark for experiencing their positive effects most strongly. Yet, as this chart shows, **only 9 percent of youth have 31 or more assets**. More than half have 20 or fewer assets. Copyright © 1997 by Search Institute; Minneapolis, MN; 800-888-7828; www.search-institute.org.

► Schools saw a way to positively address social, emotional, and psychological issues without detracting from their educational goals.

► Police officers in some communities witnessed drops in juvenile crime rates as they developed relationships with young people.

► Congregations discovered that asset building tapped into their intergenerational nature and provided a language and framework for helping adults see their roles in young peoples' lives.

► Health-care providers embraced asset building as a holistic complement to the medical services they provide.

► Business saw rises in morale and productivity when they supported their employees' involvement with families and communities.

► Cross-sector groups found that the framework of Developmental Assets provided a common language to discuss their shared goals for healthy youth (a sometimes elusive concept).

Search Institute was privileged to join these innovators on a journey through uncharted territory. In the process we have learned a great deal about what

40 Developmental Assets for Adolescents (Ages 12–18)

Search Institute has identified the following building blocks of healthy development that help young people grow up healthy, caring, and responsible.

External assets

Support
1. **Family support**—Family life provides high levels of love and support.
2. **Positive family communication**—Young person and her or his parent(s) communicate positively, and young person is willing to seek advice and counsel from parents.
3. **Other adult relationships**—Young person receives support from three or more nonparent adults.
4. **Caring neighborhood**—Young person experiences caring neighbors.
5. **Caring school climate**—School provides a caring, encouraging environment.
6. **Parent involvement in schooling**—Parent(s) are actively involved in helping young person succeed in school.

Empowerment
7. **Community values youth**—Young person perceives that adults in the community value youth.
8. **Youth as resources**—Young people are given useful roles in the community.
9. **Service to others**—Young person serves in the community one hour or more per week.
10. **Safety**—Young person feels safe at home, at school, and in the neighborhood.

Boundaries and Expectations
11. **Family boundaries**—Family has clear rules and consequences and monitors the young person's whereabouts.
12. **School boundaries**—School provides clear rules and consequences.
13. **Neighborhood boundaries**—Neighbors take responsibility for monitoring young people's behavior.
14. **Adult role models**—Parent(s) and other adults model positive, responsible behavior.
15. **Positive peer influence**—Young person's best friends model responsible behavior.
16. **High expectations**—Both parent(s) and teachers encourage the young person to do well.

Constructive Use of Time
17. **Creative activities**—Young person spends three or more hours per week in lessons or practice in music, theater, or other arts.
18. **Youth programs**—Young person spends three or more hours per week in sports, clubs, or organizations at school and/or in the community.
19. **Religious community**—Young person spends one or more hours per week in activities in a religious institution.
20. **Time at home**—Young person is out with friends "with nothing special to do" two or fewer nights per week.

Internal assets

Commitment to Learning
21. **Achievement motivation**—Young person is motivated to do well in school.
22. **School engagement**—Young person is actively engaged in learning.
23. **Homework**—Young person reports doing at least one hour of homework every school day.
24. **Bonding to school**—Young person cares about her or his school.
25. **Reading for pleasure**—Young person reads for pleasure three or more hours per week.

Positive Values
26. **Caring**—Young person places high value on helping other people.
27. **Equality and social justice**—Young person places high value on promoting equality and reducing hunger and poverty.
28. **Integrity**—Young person acts on convictions and stands up for her or his beliefs.
29. **Honesty**—Young person "tells the truth even when it is not easy."
30. **Responsibility**—Young person accepts and takes personal responsibility.
31. **Restraint**—Young person believes it is important not to be sexually active or to use alcohol or other drugs.

Social Competencies
32. **Planning and decision making**—Young person knows how to plan ahead and make choices.
33. **Interpersonal competence**—Young person has empathy, sensitivity, and friendship skills.
34. **Cultural competence**—Young person has knowledge of and comfort with people of different cultural/racial/ethnic backgrounds.
35. **Resistance skills**—Young person can resist negative peer pressure and dangerous situations.
36. **Peaceful conflict resolution**—Young person seeks to resolve conflict nonviolently.

Positive Identity
37. **Personal power**—Young person feels he or she has control over "things that happen to me."
38. **Self-esteem**—Young person reports having a high self-esteem.
39. **Sense of purpose**—Young person reports that "my life has a purpose."
40. **Positive view of personal future**—Young person is optimistic about her or his personal future.

The Power of Assets

On one level, the 40 Developmental Assets represent common wisdom about the kinds of positive experiences and characteristics that young people need and deserve. But their value extends further. Surveys of more than 200,000 students in grades 6–12 reveal that assets are powerful influences on adolescent behavior. Regardless of gender, ethnic heritage, economic situation, or geographic location, these assets both promote positive behaviors and attitudes and help protect young people from many different problem behaviors.

0–10 assets   21–30 assets
11–20 assets   31–40 assets

Promoting Positive Behaviors and Attitudes

Our research shows that the more assets students report having, the more likely they are to also report the following patterns of behavior.

Exhibits Leadership
Has been a leader of an organization or group in the past 12 months.

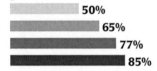

50%
65%
77%
85%

Maintains Good Health
Takes good care of body (such as eating foods that are healthy and exercising regularly).

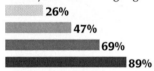

26%
47%
69%
89%

Values Diversity
Thinks it is important to get to know people of other racial/ethnic groups.

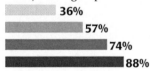

36%
57%
74%
88%

Succeeds in School
Gets mostly As on report card (an admittedly high standard).

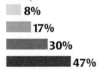

8%
17%
30%
47%

Protecting Youth from High-Risk Behaviors

Assets not only promote positive behaviors, they also protect young people: the more assets a young person reports having, the less likely he or she is to make harmful or unhealthy choices. *(Note that these definitions are set rather high, suggesting ongoing problems, not experimentation.)*

Problem Alcohol Use
Has used alcohol three or more times in the past 30 days or got drunk once or more in the past two weeks.

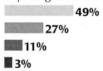

49%
27%
11%
3%

Violence
Has engaged in three or more acts of fighting, hitting, injuring a person, carrying a weapon, or threatening physical harm in the past 12 months.

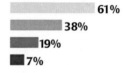

61%
38%
19%
7%

Illicit Drug Use
Used illicit drugs (marijuana, cocaine, LSD, PCP or angel dust, heroin, or amphetamines) three or more times in the past 12 months.

39%
18%
6%
1%

Sexual Activity
Has had sexual intercourse three or more times in lifetime.

32%
21%
11%
3%

it takes to initiate a broad-scope transformation effort, and have committed to working toward changes in our society's approach to nurturing young people.

Today there are more than 600 asset-building initiatives throughout North America, and several in other parts of the world. Many of them have successfully infused asset building deeply and systematically into schools, businesses, community organizations, neighborhoods, and families. We have engaged with them—observing, coaching, consulting, evaluating, and listening. We have learned a good deal about what works—and what doesn't. Here we share with you techniques sharpened on the wheel of experience. You will benefit from the collective efforts of thousands of *asset champions*—passionate and compassionate leaders who have risen to the challenge of spreading the word about the power of assets to as many people as will listen (see "Asset Champions" on page 5).

The Road Increasingly Traveled

Clearly, the 600-plus communities involved in this work have subtle and not-so-subtle differences based on population, history, geography, and so on. While there are some common denominators—desire for change, presence of asset champions, commitment by at least some additional members to children and youth—each journey is different from others. Yours will be too.

This guidebook is therefore not intended to provide you with a single asset-building itinerary. Like any good travel guide, we tell you what we think you shouldn't miss, and what you might want to try if you have the time, resources, and enthusiasm. But ultimately it's up to you to plan your destination and your route. The fun in this is that you get to do things your way. The challenge is that you'll have many choices to make—and you may not always like the results of your decisions.

To help, we share with you what we know has worked for others. With data from hundreds of thousands of young people, as well as in-depth case studies in communities with established asset-building initiatives, we know a lot about the process.

The framework on the next page presents what we've learned about the five major phases of the pathway of community change. This is a winding, not linear, route. There are many occasions when communities loop back, and when different people and organizations are at different points along the way. But while community approaches vary widely, there are consistencies in the way that change eventually comes about.

Asset Champions

Asset champions are probably much like you. They have caught the vision of asset building and are ready to take it to new levels in their communities. Some asset champions are tour guides, making all the arrangements and narrating the trip. Others are more like Sherpas; they know the territory, do the hardest work, and stay primarily behind the scenes.

Assets for Colorado Youth (ACY), a nonprofit, Denver-based organization, says that regardless of their personal style, asset champions share similar qualities:

1. A deep sense of commitment and connection to the community;
2. Social consciousness;
3. Magnetic qualities that draw people together on behalf of youth;
4. Legitimacy as social change agents and messengers;
5. Heightened awareness of teachable moments; and
6. The ability to apply asset-building concepts in ways that help others connect the asset message to their everyday lives.

Assets champions are, says ACY, "messengers who intentionally promote assets, successfully engage others in asset building, and advocate for youth—especially in forums where youth voices might rarely be heard."

(Adapted from *Creating Social Change: The Growth of a Statewide Movement*. Denver: The Colorado Trust, 2003)

Phases of the Pathway to Change

Receptivity: Being open to change. For the change process to begin, individuals, organizations, and communities must recognize and acknowledge that their young people are not getting what they need to thrive and that things need to be and can be improved. This phase reflects dissatisfaction in one's head and heart—both an understanding and a feeling of unhappiness with the status quo—and creates a willingness to consider the need for strengthening the lives of children and youth.

Awareness: Understanding the Possibilities of Change. Before individuals, organizations, or communities take action toward positive youth development, they are likely to need information that helps them think differently about the developmental needs of young people. Exposure to emotionally moving situations may help shift or reinforce the way they feel about meeting the needs of young people. In either case, they see new possibilities, feel they can make a difference, and become ready to act accordingly. In this phase, people must be convinced of the benefits of asset building and of their own capacity (time, skills, and opportunities) for personally engaging with young people and taking social action to better young people's circumstances.

Mobilization: Organizing for Change. The mobilization phase focuses on heightening individual motivation and building the teams and strategies that will prompt and sustain action to enhance young people's development. A shared vision for positive child and youth development is articulated, and individual and group action plans are created to realize it. As people and organizations commit to promoting healthy development, they may begin connecting with allies through informal networking as well as by establishing more formal coalitions.

Action: Making Change Happen. Receptivity, awareness, and mobilization do not automatically translate into intentional, sustained efforts. In the action phase, the work is about establishing a wide range of activities that fill perceived gaps in the landscape of youth and child development. This occurs through individual acts, organizational practices, and community initiatives.

Continuity: Ensuring That Change Becomes a Way of Life. Continuity emphasizes sustained momentum, energy, and progress toward healthy development for young people so that the commitment becomes woven into the fabric of personal, organizational, and community life. Continuity also addresses the challenges of keeping a developmental focus as the newness of the idea wears off and additional ideas come along. Maintaining a commitment becomes paramount.

Choosing Your Route

Different journeys are sparked by different intentions: follow-your-nose, see-the-world road trips; personal or religious pilgrimages; forced exoduses; business excursions. Similarly, we've found that there are a number of different reasons initiatives begin.

In some cases, interest in the assets bubbles up in a grassroots fashion. Perhaps a tragedy has "hit home," and people are grieving, angry, or fearful. They are looking for answers and concrete actions they can take to make a difference. Or a particular issue may have galvanized a number of like-minded thinkers who find that the assets provide a language and framework for action.

Another approach is more top down: a governing body (or bodies) identifies asset building as a priority and champions the idea, encouraging its spread throughout systems and institutions. Alternatively, there are communities where one sector, often education, embraces asset building and begins to make changes within, eventually sending feelers out into the wider community and sometimes finding enough allies to bring about wider engagement.

In some situations, two or more of these catalysts are happening at the same time, potentially leading to wonderful synergy and enthusiasm, and ultimately to sustained, positive change. Your asset-building priorities and techniques will depend on where, how, and why your asset-building journey begins. The section "Landmarks" (on page 8) shows three composite community sketches derived from the variety of communities we've worked with. That's followed later in the book by recommended techniques each community might find useful in launching, growing, and sustaining an initiative.

Culture Shock

As seasoned explorers know, *journey* is not necessarily synonymous with *vacation*. Vacation implies a break or rest, some time off. A journey, on the other hand, implies a goal and destination. It is often not relaxing or restful, and it is something that changes your life forever, not just a week or two. Regardless of how long or how far you go, the experience of journeying to and being immersed in another culture adds perspective that cannot be replicated. Sometimes when we travel we discover that home is truly where our hearts are, and we anticipate with pleasure our return. In other cases we discover that there are different ways of being and doing. Some of those "innovations" are things we want to bring with us—changes we vow to make.

"When in Rome, do as the Romans" may be a helpful reminder for you and others as you move toward new ways of thinking about yourselves and your community. Be open to the possibilities that arise as you see what other communities have done. You don't want to take it too far and interpret it as a suggestion that you just follow the crowd. Rather, it's the simple idea that asset building is about putting yourself in new situations, trying different approaches, pushing a bit beyond your comfort zones, and learning from those who are long-term residents.

It's important to know where you're coming from so that you can chose a path that gets you where you want to go. Developmental Assets give you the opportunity to find clarity about your starting point, and then envision and move toward positive change. Perhaps you'll try out another community's approach and discover that parts of it work for you.

More realistically, you'll replicate some of what other communities have done, come up with your own innovations, and stick with some of the practices that have served you well thus far.

When you are willing to take some calculated risks, you begin to imagine all kinds of new possibilities: all adults building caring relationships with children and teenagers; neighbors calling young people by name and seeking out points of connection; young people authentically engaged in civic processes and procedures.

Traveling Companions

For many years the popular thinking in our society was that youth development was the sole responsibility of parents and professionals. In growing numbers, adults and youth are rethinking that notion and embracing the idea that everyone can play a role in nurturing young people.

After years of studying community change and learning alongside communities committed to making change happen, Search Institute has named five action strategies that new and ongoing initiatives can use to guide the work they do in their own towns, cities, or regions.

Asset-building initiatives work thoughtfully to determine how people in all spheres of life can be involved. What keeps initiatives vibrant are the relationships that develop between the adults and young people in each sphere and in the networks of adults formed across those spheres.

The five action strategies provide a practical approach to identifying, encouraging, and linking all the people, places, activities, and programs necessary for a powerful collective effort. With an initiative, you can intensify your efforts to:

▶ *Engage adults* from all walks of life to develop sustained, strength-building relationships with children and adolescents, both within families and in neighborhoods.

▶ *Mobilize young people* to use their power as asset builders and change agents. This means listening to their input and including them in decision making.

▶ *Activate sectors* of the community—such as schools, congregations, businesses, youth and family services, human services, and health

Landmarks

Despite each community's unique characteristics, there are some common denominators of asset building that we have been able to identify. Below are three composite community sketches based on what we have learned about why and how communities undertake an asset-building change process.

PROFILE: Small Town

Location
Sparsely populated rural area

History
This community experienced a series of tragedies and crises over several years: the death of a beloved teacher in an alcohol-related car crash, the suicide of a student, and the closing of a local canning company. Anecdotally, parents and others are noticing an increase in alcohol and other drug use and a sense of hopelessness among young people.

First Asset Champions
▶ A pastor
▶ A number of parents
▶ A business owner
▶ The high school principal

Motivation for Beginning the Journey
People start talking about their fears that young people are struggling, that there may be more crises if nothing is done. The school principal, the business leader, and several parents all attend the pastor's church. They have different reasons for being concerned but realize they are all invested in making positive change.

Key Sectors Involved
▶ Schools
▶ Congregations

Priorities
▶ Giving people a chance to share their grief and concerns; and
▶ Introducing immediate action that people can take to feel like they are *doing* something in response to what has happened.

First Steps
Gathering people to talk, share, process, and then move into planning and goal setting. This can be accomplished through the following:
▶ Public listening sessions;
▶ Adult education time at the church;
▶ Parent meetings at the school; and
▶ A town meeting.

Roadblocks
▶ There is not a lot of institutional investment or interest.
▶ Some people are still very much in the process of healing; it is often difficult for people to move toward focusing on a positive vision.

Community Strengths
▶ An incredible passion has grown out of pain.
▶ There are lots of informal opportunities to work together.
▶ People know each other, so change can begin quickly.

How Youth Can Be Brought on Board
▶ This occurs mostly on a case-by-case basis through existing affiliations (congregations, schools, families).
▶ A youth advisory council is eventually developed when the initiative becomes established.

PROFILE: Big City

Location
Large city

History
The community has several well-established and respected youth- and family-serving organizations. There is also a strong core of active neighborhood groups. These organizations and groups tend to operate in isolation, having little or no contact with one another.

First Asset Champions
▶ Executive director of a youth organization

Motivation for Beginning the Journey
The director of one well-established, respected youth-serving organization hears about the Developmental Assets three times in a month: during a conference on best practices in youth development, in a conversation with a board member of the national office of his organization, and in a newsletter sent home from his child's school.

Key Sectors Involved
▶ Youth development professionals
▶ Neighborhood groups

Priorities
▶ Bringing the appropriate people on board early so they aren't "surprised" and potentially offended later on by shifts in the group's approach;
▶ Building trust;
▶ Establishing a vision;
▶ Setting goals; and
▶ Establishing processes and structure.

First Steps
▶ A series of meetings of youth development professionals and other stakeholders;
▶ Crafting a vision; and
▶ Conducting the Search Institute *Profiles of Student Life: Attitudes and Behaviors* survey.

Roadblocks
▶ There is a lack of parent/family involvement.
▶ It is difficult to get the ideas "to the streets."
▶ It is challenging to make it real for the front-line youth workers and young people involved in the organizations.
▶ Many different channels of communication make it difficult to ensure that the appropriate people are receiving the messages.
▶ It takes a long time to convince the schools to do the survey.

Community Strengths
▶ Formal buy-in on the part of stakeholders;
▶ Several "distribution" channels;
▶ Many groups that can reach kids; and
▶ A number of potential but untapped funded resources available.

How Youth Can Be Brought on Board
▶ To help with implementation within organizations, a cross-organization board is developed to help identify and monitor youth strengths and needs within the community.
▶ Youth can easily be involved in various events and activities that appeal to them.

PROFILE: Cross County

Location
Suburban, multi-city

History
The school district has prevention coordinators who work in the three high schools (including an alternative school) and three middle schools. There are also 12 elementary schools.

First Asset Champions
▶ A school-based prevention specialist with the help of her principal and the support of the local superintendent

Motivation for Beginning the Journey
The high school prevention coordinators learn of a grant opportunity that could bring a lot of money into the district. It is a federal grant and requires the use of an approved model, one of which is Developmental Assets. One of the coordinators heard Search Institute President Peter Benson speak at a training event and purchased copies of the *150 Ways to Show Kids You Care* poster (Search Institute, 1996) and *What Kids Need to Succeed* (Search Institute and Free Spirit Publishing, 1998). She convinces her colleagues to weave together Developmental Assets and several other prevention models for the grant proposal.

Key Sectors Involved
▶ Schools

Priorities
▶ Establishing a vision;
▶ Communicating with school staff and other stakeholders;
▶ Identifying measurable objectives; and
▶ Building a leadership team that includes young people.

First Steps
▶ The Search Institute *Profiles of Student Life: Attitudes and Behaviors* survey is done right away as a part of the grant.
▶ A youth coalition is formed (out of an existing group) to help process how to present the survey data.
▶ The coalition presents the data to young people first and invites them to help decide how to present it to parents and the wider community.

Roadblocks
▶ People balk at "doing assets" because some of the assets seem outside of appropriate educational agendas and because it is not a packaged program curriculum with instructions on how to implement it.
▶ It is difficult to change very entrenched systems within the schools.
▶ It is challenging to help teachers see this approach as helpful and not simply an additional responsibility.

Community Strengths
▶ School communication channels;
▶ Access to families; and
▶ Grant money.

How Youth Can Be Brought on Board
▶ Youth can serve as prevention peer advisors.
▶ The initiative forms youth leadership training and groups.
▶ Assets are infused into student government and other student-led groups and initiatives.

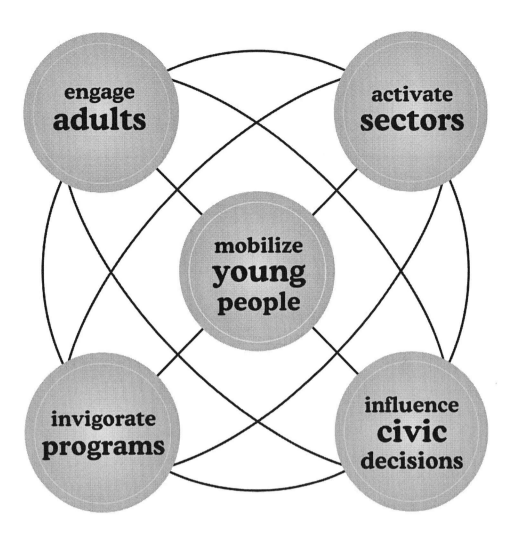

care—to create an asset-building culture and to contribute fully to young people's positive growth and development.

▶ *Invigorate programs* to become more asset rich and to be available to and accessed by all children and youth.

▶ *Influence civic decisions* by connecting with decision makers and opinion leaders to leverage financial, media, and policy resources in support of this positive transformation of communities and society.

As you think about these five action strategies, you will notice that they are not tasks to complete one by one in sequence. Instead, as you strengthen relationships within and among these spheres of influence across the community, you will build a web of interconnected efforts that reinforce one another

(See the illustration on page 9). Long-lasting success happens by merging the asset-building capacities of *all* community members—in *all* the settings where the lives of adults and youth intersect. It takes the combination of all five strategies to make lasting positive change.

Several of the techniques in this book are directly focused on engaging one person at a time. Others, like staffing and events, address the issue by looking at how organization-wide or group-wide efforts can be a means for reaching individuals. Invigorating programs, activating sectors, and influencing decisions are on one level more complex and difficult than inciting individual change. If, however, enough people catch the vision and take responsibility for asset building, these more systemic transformations become possible and even natural.

Degrees of Enthusiasm Vary

Regardless of their connections with young people, or lack thereof, most people don't adapt to change quickly or easily, even if they believe in the underlying philosophy. There will be those who will want to join you right away in your start-up work. These will most likely be people who have long been committed to the underlying ideas and positive approach of asset building. Others will be willing to come on board once they have some evidence that the idea is working and is going to stick around for a while. Still others will "discover" the movement long into the process. And a small minority may simply never be willing to entertain the idea.

There are a number of things to keep in mind, then, when reaching out beyond those early participants in asset building:

1. *Community transformation takes time.* Once you've caught the fire, you may want things to happen fast. When things aren't moving as quickly as you'd like, it's encouraging to know that asset building is cutting-edge work, and it is common for most people to be slower to get on board.

2. *It's wise to be strategic about outreach efforts.* Focus first on those who are naturally drawn to what you are doing. Then get those folks to show tentative but curious observers how great this asset-building business can be. With a critical mass, you'll eventually get to some of the more reticent folks. And don't worry about reaching every individual. Some people are simply unwilling physically or mentally to change their familiar ways.

3. *Keep the message in front of people.* All potential asset builders need to keep hearing and seeing information about the framework and the vision for your community-change destination. Latecomers in particular may not even become cognizant of the idea until you feel like you've told them a hundred times in a hundred different ways.

Not everyone wants or needs the same kind of trip. Some stop for sightseeing, meandering along; others want to quickly get to a new place and set down roots; still others hope for a guided tour. As you read and reread the town profiles, think about the similarities and differences, particularly with regard to your own community's experience. Then use the worksheet that follows, "My Community Profile" (on page 11), to help you document your reasons for getting started, the resources and challenges you are working with, and your priority techniques.

My Community Profile

	Community Name:
Location	
History	
First Asset Champions	
Motivation for Beginning the Journey	
Key Sectors Involved	
Priorities	
First Steps	
Roadblocks	
Community Strengths	
How Youth Can Be Brought on Board	

How to Use This Book

As you page through this book, you will notice a number of icons. Use these icons to identify which information is most useful to you.

Don't Miss It
In each chapter we highlight the steps that we believe, based on our experience, are critical for any initiative. Think of these as the main attractions that you won't want to bypass on your journey. Look closely, focus in clearly.

Optional Side Trips
Following the "Don't Miss It" items, there are several others that may be useful or even invaluable, depending on your situation. These "Optional Side Trips" are more specialized approaches that you may want to include in your travels.

As the Crow Flies
Look for the "As the Crow Flies" boxes to find anecdotes and specific considerations based on community type, history, or other factors.

When You Go
Whether you are embarking on a short trip or a long adventure, it is always important to make preparations. The "When You Go" sections provide background information and tips to help you make the most of your efforts.

Hit the Road

A mother we know says with enthusiasm, "Hey, guys, let's hit the road," when she really wants her children to get moving. The kids know her words mean it's time to make things happen. Similarly, we now invite you to hit the asset-building road. The resources in the next chapter will help you identify traveling companions of various ages and life stages, assess your resources, plan accordingly, and head out on your way.

Chapter 1

Charting a New Course

No matter where you start or where you're going, you need a basic plan

of how you will get from point A to point B. You don't need to necessarily map out the specific route, but it's good to know you're headed west or that you plan to use multiple means of transportation or that you'll hitch a ride with someone else. When you invest in this kind of preliminary work, you may find that things move more quickly and smoothly than you expect when it comes time to put ideas into action. If, however, you ignore, rush, or downplay this critical stage, the result may be an initiative that fizzles quickly, or never really gets going at all.

Uncovering and understanding community dynamics are a large part of what charting the course is all about. The following techniques are designed to help you do that.

Don't Miss It

- ➤ Establish an Initiator Group
- ➤ Articulate Your Vision and Mission
- ➤ Set Goals
- ➤ Assess Readiness
- ➤ Gather Input and Information
- ➤ Avoid Pitfalls
- ➤ Establish a Leadership Group
- ➤ Develop Action Plans
- ➤ Develop Communication Plans

Optional Side Trips

- ➤ Create an Infrastructure
- ➤ Integrate Assets, Prevention, and Other Priorities
- ➤ Create an Initiative Identity
- ➤ Manage Finances

Establish an Initiator Group

Even with the best resources available, mobilizing citizens for community-wide asset building is not a task for one person. You need a mix of ideas, skills, contacts, and energy from a number of asset champions who are willing to take the lay of the land, plot a course, and determine whether the journey you're considering is a feasible undertaking.

In some communities, an initiator group forms because one person catches the vision of asset building. In St. Anthony Village, Minnesota, Pastor Glenn Seefeldt became excited about assets and their impact. He identified key leaders in the community who he thought might share his interest, and he convened an initiator group.

Other communities have existing groups that discover the assets and see a connection to their current efforts. Such was the case in Cherry Creek, Colorado, where the Parent Information Network (PIN) had been focused since the 1970s on substance abuse and other risk behavior prevention. After being exposed to the asset framework, PIN realized asset building was a great strategy that would enhance what it was already doing. Today the group has morphed into Community Asset Project, Inc., or CAP, Inc. In addition to engaging parents, says Coordinator Brenda Holben, CAP builds committed community partnerships that promote Developmental Assets, ensuring all children maximize their life skills and academic

As the Crow Flies

Working in smaller communities often brings the benefit of knowing most of the key players in the area. Initiatives based in big cities or counties, on the other hand, need to be intentional about asking everyone, "Who else should know about this? Who else should be involved?"

potential. The group's 40 members include law enforcement, educators, parents, business owners, and youth.

Start with Potential Allies

The Mosaic Youth Center is a youth-led initiative in the suburbs of Minneapolis. In its book *Step by Step: A Young Person's Guide to Positive Community Change* (Search Institute, 2001), the center included a simple worksheet used to help identify people to potentially bring on board (the center calls them *potential allies*). A modified version of this worksheet "Initiator Group Recruiting Ideas" is on page 15. You may want to adapt it further by adding columns for past experience, age, and other unique and important characteristics.

When You Go

Regardless of how initiator groups form, they tend to be somewhat informal and to engage in a creative, visionary manner rather than in a task- and deadline-oriented manner. This is due, in large part, to the primary task of this group: to determine whether an asset-building initiative is feasible and desirable.

Whether you already have a number of people involved or just one or two championing the asset framework, there are some questions to consider. Which influential people would you like to try to recruit? Does or should your group represent the diversity of your community? How large should your group be? What is your primary agenda (e.g., do you want to end up being a leadership team, too, or are you just getting this going)?

Anyone in a community can be a part of an initiator group. It's best, of course, if members are enthusiastic about asset building and see the potential for it to enhance the community and its residents. Beyond that, it's a good idea to involve key leaders who can help guide the process in ways that will work well in the community, and who can leverage resources and cultivate buy-in. Some of these key leaders may be young people who are already recognized as influential. It is important to have at least several young people involved at this point.

In fact, you'll notice throughout this manual that

Initiator Group Recruiting Ideas

Name	Contact information	Why we want this person on board	What this person might get out of it	Who could help us contact this person
Kevin Baker	999-999-999 (phone)	He's the high school principal so he has influence in young people's lives and is recognized in the community. Most people respect him and his work.	A safer school, students who are better prepared to learn, support from parents and others for the work of the school.	Jesse knows him well and will ask him if we can schedule a short informational meeting after school next week.

we frequently mention potential roles for young people. We believe, and we have learned this from communities, that asset-building change cannot happen deeply and systemically if young people are not actively engaged. Engaged goes far beyond involved. Engaged implies that young people believe in asset building, take responsibility for it, and see themselves as valued and valuable influencers in the community.

It's also important to consider the balance of skills, personalities, and perspectives of the people involved. A strong initiator group typically includes a visionary, a planner, a networker, and a manager. In addition, it's helpful to have a person or two who can ask tough questions and voice doubts. To be effective, these and other members need clear communication and senses of openness and trust. Though your main focus will be the task at hand, in keeping with the overarching philosophy of asset building you'll want to spend time building, and strengthening relationships.

Questions to Consider

▶ Do you have a group whose members consider themselves initiators of an asset-building initiative? If not, who should be invited to join you?

▶ How big do you want your initiator group to be?

▶ Do you have the right mix of people? If not, what skills, interests, or perspectives would you like to add?

▶ What are your main objectives? Background research? Coalition building? Recruiting leadership group members?

▶ What kind of a commitment do you hope for or expect from your initiators?

For More Information

Step by Step: A Young Person's Guide to Positive Community Change (Search Institute, 2001).

Articulate Your Vision and Mission

Asset building is vision- and mission-driven work. A vision is a picture of where you want to go; a mission is about how you will get there. For your initiative that will likely mean that your vision will describe what you hope life will be like for young people and in your community as a whole. Your mission will briefly and concisely describe your initiative, what you do to achieve the vision, and why you're doing it.

Putting It in Writing

Often groups or organizations articulate their visions and missions in *vision statements* and *mission statements*. Formalizing your intent in this way ensures that everyone is hearing the same thing about what you are all about. For example:

> *It is our vision to have everyone in our community demonstrate in words and actions that we love, value, and appreciate each other and our young people and recognize that they are our future.*
> HC • HY of Northwest Georgia

> *The Connecticut Assets Network envisions people living in communities where everyone is a resource and makes a difference.*
> The Connecticut Assets Network (C.A.N.)

> *Our Vision is to create caring and safe communities in which young people thrive. Our Mission is to positively influence children and youth by changing the way communities raise young people.*
> Assets for Colorado Youth (ACY)

When You Go

When you know what you're working toward, it's easier to know how to get there. So when you're ready to put into words what you're about, begin with creating your vision statement. Focus on possibilities, not problems. Encourage people to dream big and to think beyond what is practical. If some group members find this difficult, remind them of efforts that have been accomplished in your community even though they initially seemed unlikely or even impossible.

The activity that follows was designed by trainer and consultant I. Shelby Andress to help walk communities through the visioning process.

Crafting a Vision

Use these steps to create a vision statement:

1. Ask group members to dream about what an ideal asset-building community would look like. Ask: "If visitors came from out of state and asked you to describe what life here is like for children and teens, what would you want to be able to say?"
2. Ask participants to draw pictures of and/or write down their descriptions.
3. Invite each person to share her/his vision. Make a list of key words, phrases, or images.
4. Sort the words, phrases, and images into several key themes.
5. Ask each person to indicate her/his top five priorities by "starring" the words, phrases, and images. Each can give five stars for her/his first priority, four stars for their second, and so on.
6. Tally the stars and choose the top three to five items to use to create your vision statement.

As you complete the six steps, use these techniques for keeping the process on track:

▶ Encourage individuals to think big, to dream about what they'd really love to be a part of—even if it doesn't feel practical.
▶ Start with brainstorming. Don't openly critique any of the ideas (and try not to judge them in your mind). Write them all down.
▶ Take an asset-building approach. Focus on positive opportunities rather than obstacles or problems. Identify what you want, not what you don't want.
▶ Work to articulate simply what your vision is. Keep it between 25 and 40 words.
▶ Be sure your group is intergenerational. Your vision will be stronger if you include young people, young adults, middle-aged adults, and elders.

For people who have already worked in youth development, creating community-wide asset-building visions sometimes comes quite easily, but not always. It can be difficult to think outside of the constraints of what we're used to or what we think is possible. The handout "A Vision of Possibility" (on page 18) lists bold images that can help you explore the widest range of possibilities for what your community could become. These are simply intended to spark ideas and push you to think outside your normal expectations.

Moving Toward Mission

Once you have a clear vision, your mission can emerge. Your mission statement should be easy to understand, brief, and concrete. People should be able to memorize and recite it. It should include *who* you are, *what* you do (or want to do), and *for whom* you want to do it.

Deciding whom to include in the process is a good first step. Keep in mind that the mission statement for your initiator group may be quite different from the one that is eventually adopted by the initiative as a whole. It's also completely acceptable to revise mission statements once you have some experience and a better sense of the path you are on.

While a mission statement should be short, its creation should be taken seriously because it will likely stay with you for a while, and be something people will come to associate with your group and with asset building in your community. Include then, in the process, people who will be working with you as well as members of your desired "audience."

You may want to start with a brainstorming session (no censoring or evaluation, just a true exchange of ideas). If necessary, break into smaller teams for a while and then report back to the larger group. The larger group can give feedback and narrow down the choices. Once you have a few selections that are acceptable to your leadership, you can run those ideas past constituents or audience members.

A Vision of Possibility

Mobilize Young People

Young people take personal responsibility for building assets and feel empowered to do so for themselves and with their peers.

- ► All young people understand their personal capacity to promote Developmental Assets for themselves and for other children and youth.
- ► Many young people seek to be involved in positive activities and relationships in their homes, neighborhoods, schools, and communities.
- ► Many youth are regularly engaged in service to others and to the community. Reflection and learning are key components of these activities.
- ► Youth model and articulate their values for peers, younger children, and adults.
- ► Youth speak out on decisions that impact their communities.

Engage Adults

Adults take personal responsibility for and feel empowered to build assets for and with young people.

- ► All adults believe in their capacity to promote Developmental Assets.
- ► All adults take responsibility for building assets for and with youth.
- ► Adults seek young people's input into decisions that impact the community.
- ► Adults expect and support other adults' positive interactions and relationships with young people.
- ► Parents let other adults know that they welcome and appreciate support.
- ► Adults model and articulate their values.
- ► Adults listen to children and youth.

Invigorate Programs

Groups and organizations throughout the community make their programs more asset rich. Programs are available and accessible to all children and youth.

- ► Schools place priority on becoming caring environments for all students, providing challenging and engaging curriculum, providing opportunities for nurturing values deemed crucial by the community, expanding and strengthening co-curricular activities, and using their connections with families to reinforce the importance of family attention to assets.
- ► Youth- and family-serving organizations train leaders and volunteers in asset-building strategies and provide meaningful opportunities for youth to serve their communities and build citizenship and leadership skills.
- ► Faith communities mobilize their capacity for intergenerational relationships, family education and support, structured time for youth, values development, leadership development, and service to the community.

Activate Sectors

Groups and organizations network with other similar organizations for learning, support, and action.

- ► Organizations collaborate within and across sectors to develop shared visions for asset building.
- ► Organizations link with other organizations within and across sectors to reduce conflicts and competition and to maximize resources such as transportation, facilities, and training.
- ► Businesses encourage and empower employees, clients, and customers to build assets—on and off the job.

Influence Civic Decisions

Developmental Assets are a regular topic of conversation throughout the community and are articulated as a community priority.

- ► A vision rooted in Developmental Assets is communicated several times a year to all residents.
- ► New residents are quickly introduced to the community's vision.
- ► Residents demand an investment in systems of clubs, teams, and organizations that provide support and resources for young people.
- ► Voters approve measures to improve schools, strengthen community opportunities for young people, and taking other youth-friendly actions.
- ► Local government—through policy, influence, training, and resource allocation—moves asset development and community-wide cooperation to top priorities.
- ► The media regularly communicate the community's vision, support mobilization efforts, and provide forums for sharing innovative actions.

Appreciative Inquiry

Appreciative inquiry, a strategy developed by David Cooperrider of Case Western Reserve University, is a unique interviewing technique that frames questions in a positive light. This can be a powerful tool for connecting young people with caring adults and for initiating community change. It's adaptable for many different kinds of groups—parent groups, citywide initiatives, a neighborhood meeting, a congregation outreach program, or a school-based project. Designed to mobilize change through a constructive, strength-based process rather than through criticism and negativity, it can involve hundreds or even thousands of people.

This concept can be especially useful for working on the mission or vision of a group. When you interview young people and adults to gather input from your community, try to frame your questions to elicit positive ideas for change. Here are some sample questions to use:

➤ What do you value about our community?
➤ What do you value about yourself as a community member?
➤ Describe something positive that has happened in the community. What made it possible?
➤ What kind of change would make the community a better place to live?
➤ What can you do to contribute to this positive change?

Instead of focusing on community problems or deficits, appreciative inquiry allows you to investigate hopeful possibilities for the future.

Questions to Consider

➤ Who should be involved in naming your vision for your community?
➤ Are there helpful examples of vision and mission statements from other initiatives or from organizations within your community?
➤ Do you need both a vision and mission statement?
➤ Who are you?
➤ Whom do you hope to reach or serve?
➤ What resources or services do you provide?
➤ How do you ensure that you listen to the voices of young people during this process?

For More Information

To learn more about appreciative inquiry, visit http://appreciativeinquiry.cwru.edu.

As the Crow Flies

Articulating vision and mission can take much longer than anticipated. It's not unusual for people to get caught up in debating short phrases, or even individual words. When this happens, it's important to distinguish between "wordsmithing" and genuine disputes over meaning. It usually works to ask the parties involved to explain the root of their concerns. Generally this will reveal the source of the problem and allow the group to move to a solution. If, however, the conversation continues and no agreement can be reached, it's sometimes better to table the issue and come back to it at a later date.

Set Goals

A goal is a clear statement describing your desired outcome—the end you are working toward. Goals typically come out of vision statements and lead to action plans. Some are organizational, focused on your group and your work together; others are programmatic, emphasizing the work upon which you are collectively focused. All goals should be specific and attainable.

Establishing clear, shared goals is important for many reasons: It's more likely that all involved will be working toward the same end (despite having different means of getting there). It helps you communicate to others what your initiative is all about. It gives you touchstones by which to measure success.

In addition to goals, initiatives often identify measurable outcomes (or short-term goals) by which they assess progress. This provides the opportunity to experience quick success while working toward more systemic change. You can begin by setting goals and then identifying objectives, or it can work the other way around. In some cases it works well to establish goals that extend over a longer period of time than your objectives. You can then periodically assess your objectives and revise them as necessary or appropriate.

The Goal Is to Take the Time

The Take the Time Initiative in Portland, Oregon, identified three overarching goals:

1. Every child will have regular contact with a caring, responsible adult who provides guidance, support, and high expectations.
2. Every child will have the opportunity to contribute to his or her community, whether through community service, participation in community decision-making processes, serving in leadership roles, or serving as a mentor to other young people.
3. All children receive a consistent message that they are valued by the adults in their community.

When You Go

A key to establishing effective goals and objectives is to have high but realistic expectations Consider how your goals relate to and grow out of your mission and vision, whether your goals are attainable, if they are focused on positive outcomes, and how you will know when you have achieved them. You'll also want to think in advance about how your goals will be evaluated throughout the life of your initiative. While many people think of evaluation as something that comes at the "end" of an effort, it ought to be integrated from the beginning. Chapter 4 has additional information on how goals can be linked to outcomes to form the basis for evaluation.

One method for establishing goals is known as creating a *logic model.* A logic model clarifies and summarizes what you plan to accomplish, as well as some of the intermediate steps and the resources you will need. You can read more about logic models in Chapter 4. For now you can use the worksheets "Setting Goals" (on page 21) and "Achieving Goals" (on page 22) to articulate your long-term goals.

Down the road you can add additional information to help report on your initiative's progress.

The first worksheet, "Setting Goals," is helpful for initiatives that are designed to last three or more years, and that have short-term as well as big-picture desired outcomes. Working back from year 5, or ahead from year 1, identify your short- and longer-term goals for your initiative.

The next worksheet, "Achieving Goals," is useful for setting goals that can be accomplished in one year or less and for mapping out the actions that you are planning to take to achieve those goals. It can be used individually or in combination with "Setting Goals." Make sure the steps lead logically to the outcomes.

Questions to Consider

▶ How do your goals connect with your vision and mission?
▶ Are all of the goals attainable?
▶ Are you pushing yourselves enough?
▶ Are you focused on positive outcomes?
▶ How will you know when you get there? What will have happened?

As the Crow Flies
Beware of the lure of unattainable goals. Your vision should be idealistic, but your goals need to be grounded in reality. It's especially tempting to inflate goals when seeking funding. Making the case, for example, that asset-building efforts will lead to improved test scores among students is doable on paper but incredibly difficult to demonstrate. More reasonable expectations might be to see increases in students' enthusiasm for reading and reported loyalty to their schools.

Setting Goals

Action Strategy	Year 1 Goals	Year 2 Goals	Year 3 Goals	Year 4 Goals	Year 5 Goals
Engage Adults					
Mobilize Young People					
Invigorate Programs					
Activate Sectors					
Influence Civic Decisions					

Achieving Goals

Goal	Steps and actions we will take to accomplish this goal	How these steps will help us accomplish this goal	How we will measure progress

Assess Readiness

In our work on examining and articulating the change pathway, we learned a lot about what it means to be ready for change. In some communities, such as the small town profiled earlier on page 8, it's clear that there is a need or strong desire for change and that asset building is a strong potential approach. In others, a number of people get excited about assets but the groundswell of interest and enthusiasm just isn't there.

To be ready for change means, in part, that there is among a core group of people a sense of dissatisfaction with the way things are. True readiness also requires energy and enthusiasm, because while change can be exciting and invigorating, there is no doubt that it also requires patience, commitment, and work.

Before getting to the point of assessing readiness, most asset champions have already established that there is some level of desire for change within a community. The big question is whether that desire is strong enough and spread widely enough to support a community effort. You'll also want to consider factors such as local history, existing efforts, available resources, leaders, and knowledge of and support for asset building.

Your initial steps should include bringing together key stakeholders—people who would have something to gain or lose in the outcome of an asset-building initiative. Depending on their knowledge of the Developmental Assets framework, you can inform them appropriately about your ideas and the emerging plans for asset building. Then take time to hear their perspectives, questions, and concerns related to readiness.

Mapping

Mapping is a tool that you can use for many things, including assessing readiness. The basic process is to start with a concept, idea, or question, and draw links to that starting point. The Waupaca Healthy Community • Healthy Youth initiative in Wisconsin, for example, used mapping to document existing community resources that supported asset building. It discovered that while adults identified area parks, congregations, schools, and the library as likely places for young people to gather, youth said they actually got together at the local truck stop and community parking lots. Another asset-building initiative, the Mosaic Youth Center (Robbinsdale, Minnesota), developed the sample map that follows:

Mapping Example: Reducing Fighting through Peer Mediation

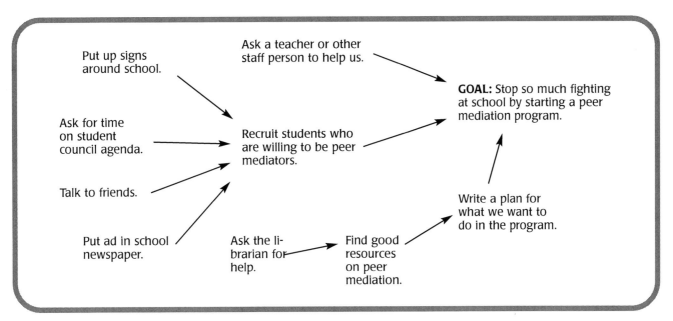

Source: adapted from *Step by Step: A Young Person's Guide to Positive Community Change* by The Mosaic Youth Center Board of Directors with Jennifer Griffin-Wiesner. Copyright © 2001 by Search Institute, Minneapolis, Minnesota; 800-888-7828; www.search-institute.org.

When You Go

It's usually a challenge to convince a large group of people to let go of the status quo, "the way things have always been." And it takes time.

In his book *All Kids Are Our Kids,* Search Institute President Peter Benson describes 12 often-entrenched attitudes that many communities must shift in order to become more attentive to young people's developmental needs. While they may not all apply directly to you, it is important to be aware of others' perceptions or beliefs in these 12 areas and to remember that these culture shifts take time.

Culture shift #1: From youth as objects to youth as actors. Young people have tremendous influence on and potential for asset building. They can form relationships, model healthy values and commitments, reinforce boundaries, and contribute in other ways to community life. Tapping this under-recognized resource not only strengthens young people's own asset bases, but also deepens the pool of resources available for community mobilization.

Culture shift #2: From deficit language to asset language. In many cultures adolescence has come to be viewed as a stressful, conflict-ridden time. Parents dread it; teens cannot wait to get out of it. But the Developmental Asset framework frees us from that false notion by focusing on teenagers' strengths and serves as a reminder of what an exciting and wonderful time adolescence can be. Yes, adolescents are maturing at a remarkable rate.

Yes, they take risks, and yes, they can be moody and unpredictable. But they also have an incredible capacity to serve others; they need and desire to have positive, supportive relationships with parents and other adults; and they have the ability to contribute to community life in new and wonderful ways.

Seeing teens this way requires shifts at both the personal and social levels toward viewing young people as full of promise and possibility, much the way many people see babies and toddlers (who, interestingly, are also maturing quickly, taking risks, and acting rather moody and unpredictable).

Culture shift #3: From some children and youth to all children and youth. It's easier to focus on youth at both ends of the "need" spectrum than it is to provide for the majority who land in the middle. On one end of the continuum are young people

whom we identify as most at risk because of health issues, family circumstances, or other factors. On the other end are young people who seem to have it all: multiple kinds of intelligence, good looks, charisma, and other characteristics that draw attention and interest. But the reality is that nearly all children and adolescents need more Developmental Assets than they now have.

Systems of support, boundaries and expectations, constructive time use, values socialization, and competency building are too fragile for too many young people. So while it is certainly crucial to pay special attention to those who appear to suffer the most, and to provide stimulating and challenging environments for those whose gifts and strengths are obvious, the central challenge is to reclaim the kind of community-wide attention to positive development that will benefit *all* young people.

Culture shift #4: From early childhood only to the first two decades of life. In addition to expanding our focus "out" to include young people from all walks of life, the Developmental Assets framework calls on us to think "up" and recognize that early childhood is not the only critical developmental stage. Each phase of childhood and adolescence requires persistent attention to assets. Each one builds on experiences, positive or negative, from the one prior. Asset-building efforts will be most effective when they are built on this broad developmental perspective.

Culture shift #5: From age segregation to intergenerational integration. From a "kids' table" at family dinners to political battles over social security, we are too often divided by age and generation. The result is a startling and unhealthy lack of sustained relationships between unrelated elders and youth.

Culture shift #6: From self-interest to shared responsibility. Many people believe that it's a good idea for adults to develop positive relationships with young people. Those beliefs, however, don't always lead to action. An important step in creating an asset-rich environment for young people is to change the norms so that all residents in the community understand, believe in, and act on their responsibility for young people. Each and every young person should experience many formal and informal supportive interactions on a daily basis. That can only happen if many adults take action.

Culture shift #7: From a focus on programs to a focus on relationships. Youth workers, teachers, and others who have committed their professional lives to working with children and youth deserve a great deal of respect and gratitude for that decision. They cannot, however, be expected to pick up the ball when others drop it. Asset building is not a matter of hiring more professionals and starting new programs. Rather, it calls on asset champions to work to activate and enhance the capacity of community members to care for young people, communicate expectations and boundaries, model and affirm desired social behavior, nurture educational commitments and a love of learning, and articulate and live out positive values.

Culture shift #8: From a fragmented agenda to a unifying vision. Implicit in many of the first seven shifts is the need to move from fragmented, competitive agendas to a unifying vision for children and adolescents. If all socializing systems in a community share a commitment to a vision of healthy development, each can see its own niche in the larger vision. Everyone doesn't have to do everything, but all realize they are on the same team. The uniting vision of asset building calls for shared action on a community-wide basis, but it also challenges individuals and institutions within the community to examine their own priorities and programs to determine how they build assets and what they can do to be more effective in contributing to the larger community vision.

Culture shift #9: From conflicting signals to consistent messages. Mixed messages can be one of the most confusing, frustrating, and destructive aspects of adolescence. As young people work through questions about their own identity and place in the word, they hear and see things that don't make sense together: teens are young and sexy vs. abstinence is the only safe choice; drugs are bad vs. smoking is cool and alcohol is fun and glamorous; boys need to be tough vs. don't be a bully; girls are spiteful and malicious toward one another vs. a friend is someone you can always count on. Unless socializing systems share a script about what is inbounds and out-of-bounds, about values and expectations (integrity, honesty, fairness, respect, justice, caring, and academic motivation), youth have a hard time finding solid ground on which to stand when they make decisions and figure out who they are and what they want to be.

Culture shift # 10: From efficiency to redundancy. The word redundancy has developed a bad reputation. It is often maligned as a source of economic waste. Streamlined efficiency requires eliminating redundancy. In raising healthy young people, however, the need is different. Redundancy is in fact essential. Developmentally attentive communities provide multiple exposures to the Developmental Assets, and there really is not—nor should there be—an efficient way to do this. Building and living relationships—the core of asset building—cannot be streamlined.

Culture shift #11: From short-term priorities to long-term commitment. A problem-centered focus perpetuates a cultural tendency to shift attention and priorities from one issue to the next, depending on whatever is foremost in public consciousness. We design programs with goals to "reduce (insert problem) by (insert percent) by (insert year), when the funding runs out." The Developmental Assets framework provides a foundation for long-term action based on the importance of ongoing, positive relationships and opportunities across at least the first two decades of life. Within this larger vision there are opportunities for focused, time-limited activities that contribute to the larger vision.

Culture shift #12: From civic disengagement to engagement. This shift challenges the widespread (if rarely articulated) assumption that people are primarily—or perhaps only—responsible for their own lives and those of their family members. If we are to succeed in activating all residents and sectors for a sustained and unified commitment to young people, several additional shifts must occur simultaneously. One is to move from an overdependence on schools for addressing human development issues to a place where schools are working in concert with asset-

As the Crow Flies

Readiness does not have a particular size or shape. Like water, it adjusts to fit the space of the vessel in which it is contained. In a community that has experienced tragedy, readiness may be passionate and impatient. When an initiative emerges from a school setting, the sense of readiness may feel more enthusiastic and full of anticipation and camaraderie.

building neighbors, families, congregations, youth organizations, and employers. A second shift is moving from the isolation of family to the integration of family within community.

As part of your readiness assessment, consider asking your initiator group, leadership group, or other key stakeholders to reflect on these shifts and where your community lands on each continuum.

Two resources that might be helpful in assessing readiness are those on the following pages. They are designed as discussion starters. Individuals in your initiator group and others you contact can complete one or both of them independently before talking as a group about your reactions. This will help you all begin to see your community's strengths, areas that need particular attention, and potential action steps.

Questions to Consider

▶ What asset-building strengths does your community have to build on?

▶ What needs in the community will your initiative address?

▶ What is already happening to address these needs? Would your initiative complement or conflict with existing efforts?

▶ Have there been efforts in the past to address these needs? How successful were they?

▶ Who in the community should be involved from the beginning to increase the likelihood of your initiative's credibility and success?

▶ Who in the community might emerge as an asset champion and be willing to do the necessary organizing, networking, and planning?

▶ What resistance might you expect?

For More Information

Building Community from the Inside Out: A Path Toward Finding and Mobilizing a Community's Assets by John P. Kretzmenn and John L. McKnight (Chicago: ACTA Publications, 1993; available from Search Institute).

Visible Thinking: Unlocking Causal Mapping for Practical Business Results by Fran Ackermann, John M. Bryson, Colin Eden, and Charles Finn (Ontario: WileyCanada, 2004). Note: One of the authors of this book, John Bryson, has written a number of resources specifically for nonprofit and public

agencies. Some of these, such as *Leadership for the Common Good: Tackling Public Problems in a Shared-Power World* (San Francisco: Jossey-Bass, 1992; co-authored with Barbara C. Crosby), include information about mapping in these environments.

All Kids Are Our Kids: What Communities Must Do to Raise Caring and Responsible Children and Adolescents (San Francisco: Jossey-Bass, 1997).

Gather Input and Information

In addition to determining readiness, there are things you'll want to learn as your initiative evolves. There may also be other information you want right now. That's a good sign. Indeed, the most effective initiatives are those whose champions listen and observe well. They are always in "information-gathering mode," talking with stakeholders, watching interactions, and visiting programs and people.

Gathering to Listen

There are many ways to listen, including discussion groups, one-on-one interviews in person or on the phone, public forums, Internet exchanges, telephone hotlines, and surveys. Many communities gather citizens and engage them in dialogue with asset-building innovators listening to the conversations.

Residents who initiated the Moorhead Healthy Community Initiative in Minnesota, for example, first came together with leaders to discuss concerns over news reports of escalating crime. The talks led to a highly successful asset-building effort.

Similarly, the mayor and city manager of Hampton, Virginia, originally convened a community meeting to discuss an economic development initiative. Asset building emerged as a priority after the discussion turned to the future of the community's workforce.

Community-wide and even some statewide youth or youth-adult summits have been held in British Columbia, Kansas, Ohio, Nevada, North Dakota, Wisconsin, and many other locations. Town meetings are also becoming common as well. These and other strategies are valid and valuable because gathering input is an exploratory, not evaluative, process.

Assessing Community Readiness for Asset Building: Part I

	Yes	No	I don't know
1. Is there a history of commitment to children and youth in your community?			
2. Is there a history of successful collaboration and/or community-wide action?			
3. Are there other community-wide issues, initiatives, or efforts that will vie for citizens' time and energy?			
4. Are a variety of sectors involved in assessing the feasibility of an asset-building initiative?			
5. Are young people actively involved in launching an asset-building initiative?			
6. Have you and your fellow asset champions worked to create a shared vision for your community?			
7. Are the people and organizations involved passionate and excited about the Developmental Assets framework?			
8. Are the individuals and organizations involved becoming empowered to build assets for and with young people?			
9. Do the people involved represent the diversity of your community (in terms of age, ethnicity, gender, income, religious beliefs, and so on)?			
10. Are the people involved beginning to use the language of Developmental Assets without being prompted to do so?			
11. Have you addressed issues of inclusiveness and diversity?			
12. Do you have access to funding or other financial support?			
13. Do you sense that your community is ready to rally together behind your children and youth?			

Assessing Community Readiness for Asset Building: Part II

<table>
<tr>
<td>1. Where do you live, and what type of community do you have? (Consider physical geography and the legal boundaries, as well as geography of influence—how boundaries impact systems, functions, and interactions.)</td>
<td></td>
</tr>
<tr>
<td>2. What issues are most important in your community? (The economy? Population growth or change? Education?)</td>
<td></td>
</tr>
<tr>
<td>3. What's already working well? (Consider youth-serving organizations, congregations, school programs, and individuals who take action to nurture children and youth.)</td>
<td></td>
</tr>
<tr>
<td>4. How is your initiative organized? Are you "bubbling up" in informal ways, thanks to some very committed people? Are you connected to a particular program or organization? Has a formal community-wide coalition been formed?</td>
<td></td>
</tr>
<tr>
<td>5. Should you administer the Search Institute Profiles of Student Life: Attitudes and Behaviors survey? (Would it help generate interest? Do you have other baseline data on your young people? Have you conducted the survey in the past?)</td>
<td></td>
</tr>
</table>

When You Go

There is a unique opportunity during the early stages of an asset-building initiative to learn from community members about their hopes, perceptions of current realities, and strategies they think might work to bring about needed change. You'll have the most success gathering information if you make it *easy* and *desirable* for people to participate. You'll be asking them to do something that is outside their normal routines (and probably outside of what they typically think about) so reducing the level of inconvenience raises the possibility of participation. That can mean offering transportation, providing a snack or meal, scheduling several gatherings in different locations, or thanking people for their time with incentives like coupons for local merchants.

You can use the simple worksheet, "Identifying Community Asset-Building Strengths and Challenges" (on page 30), to gather information about your community from many different people and groups. It may be most effective when used as a discussion starter, but you could also ask people to fill it out and return it.

Questions to Consider

➤ What issues are important to your community?
➤ How do people who live here describe your community? How about those who work or recreate here but don't live here? Is it important to hear from them as well?
➤ What's already working well? What makes you proud of or happy about living here?
➤ Are there things you should be aware of or concerned about related to asset building?
➤ How can you organize your initiative in a way that most people will support it?
➤ Should you survey your young people using Search Institute surveys?

For More Information

Search Institute Survey Services, 800-888-7828; www.search-institute.org/surveys/.

Avoid Pitfalls

While no strategy for starting an initiative has been deemed the most effective, watching initiatives build (or fail to build) momentum has led us to see potential pitfalls to avoid. In many cases problems arise when leaders take extreme approaches to one or more aspects of community change.

Language Issues

Greg Ryan has been told more than once that he shouldn't use the term *assets* when describing the youth development work of his organization. "It's confusing," people tell him. "It sounds like you're speaking of a financial institution." But Ryan, coordinator of the Connecticut Assets Network (CAN), has stuck with the Developmental Assets language, arguing that the purpose for CAN's existence is to shed light on this concept. Now he says that the word is becoming widely used across his state as well as the nation to describe opportunities and qualities that allow us to become caring and contributing members of our communities.

As the Crow Flies

Some people are very comfortable speaking up in public or group settings. Others prefer sharing their ideas and opinions in private conversations or even putting their thoughts in writing. No matter what the characteristics are of your community, you'll yield a more complete picture if you build in different listening mechanisms.

Identifying Community Asset-Building Strengths and Challenges

	Strengths	Challenges	Opportunities	Concerns
Support: Young people have positive communication and relationships with families, peers, schools, neighborhoods, and community.				
Empowerment: Young people are safe and know that they are valued and valuable.				
Boundaries and Expectations: Parents, teachers, and others have high yet realistic expectations and standards for behavior.				
Constructive Use of Time: Young people have a good balance of time spent in school, in out-of-school activities, and at home.				
Commitment to Learning: The joy and importance of learning are communicated to and modeled for young people.				
Positive Values: Shared, positive values are openly talked about, nurtured, and lived.				
Social competencies: Young people have many opportunities to develop interpersonal strengths such as resistance skills, planning and decision-making, and appreciation of diversity.				
Positive identity: The future looks promising and bright to young people, and they believe they have power over their own lives.				

When You Go

It's easy to fall into the trap of wanting to water down or avoid the asset language if it's new in your community. But if you are really committed to the concept, then using the term *Developmental Assets* is an important piece of the puzzle, because using consistent language helps foster shared understanding and mutual commitment to concepts and ideas. The handout "Maintaining Balance in an Asset-Building Initiative" (on page 32) shows other examples of extreme approaches to some critical aspects of initiative development.

Questions to Consider

▶ Where are you now on these continua?

▶ What areas are the easiest for you to balance?

▶ What gives you the most trouble?

▶ What issues do you need to address to avoid these pitfalls?

▶ Are there disagreements or points of contention that need to be addressed regarding these issues?

Establish a Leadership Group

A leadership group generally emerges from an initiator group after the initiator group has determined that an asset-building initiative is feasible and desirable. The leadership group carries out the vision and direction of the initiative. It takes on responsibility for designing and implementing a community-wide plan.

There are many different types of leaders. Often, the most effective leadership groups include a mix of people who recognize and appreciate their own strengths and those of their comrades. For example, your group may include a visionary who keeps the big picture of your efforts in front of everyone, a connector who knows and communicates with many people in the community, a young person who knows how to make things happen with other youth, an elder who has seen similar efforts succeed or fail in the past, and an organizer who keeps people focused and on track.

Diversity of all types is worth pursuing, even though it's sometimes easier to stay within familiar

circles. To truly make a difference at the community-wide level, you need leaders who are familiar with, connected to, and respected by the majority of community members. Who those people are of course depends on your community. As a general rule, it's wise to at least strive for people from different life stages, schools, career/life paths, sexes, ethnicities, religions, areas of expertise, and income levels.

That said, diverse groups pose their own challenges. Styles may conflict, spoken or unspoken biases may influence interactions, and priorities may differ. You can deal with this in part by staying focused on your mission of making a positive difference for *all* young people, and by dedicating time to building trust.

Recruiting leaders can also be a challenge, particularly if you are forming a new group rather than building on one that is established and known in the community. Recruiting is best done one-on-one with an emphasis on why you want each individual involved. Telling people you'd like them to be involved because they have communications skills and expert-

As the Crow Flies

It can be relatively easy to avoid the most blatant and extreme pitfalls when building an initiative. More insidious are the subtle acts that erode trust or efficacy over time. Stereotypes can have a lot to do with that. In suburban communities, for example, there may be an assumption that most people are on the same economic playing field and therefore will have access to computers. Scheduling all events via e-mail may seem efficient and sufficient, but will leave out those who don't have easy access. Smaller communities may feel less need than others to do outreach, thereby leaving out "newcomers" and others who have traditionally been disengaged. And in big cities a lot of time might be spent "getting people on board," so much so that early supporters may lose interest or begin to feel unappreciated.

Maintaining Balance in an Asset-Building Initiative

As with many aspects of life, *all things in moderation* is a good rule of thumb. We recommend reviewing this sheet periodically and checking in with your leaders and constituents on how balanced you are on these issues.

Structure

It is possible to develop a rigid organizational plan that, while perhaps clear, can get in the way of creativity, growth, or innovation.

An initiative might instead keep things so loose it's difficult to know the priorities, and even more challenging to know how to get involved or take action.

Turf

It's tempting, if you dislike conflict, to simply disregard or ignore potential turf issues.

The other extreme, though, is equally hazardous: obsessing about turf issues to the extent that people hold back out of fear of offending or alienating someone or some group.

Flair

Some initiatives put all their efforts into initial big events or awareness-raising campaigns, but then fail to develop substance and depth that keeps people engaged.

Other groups focus so heavily on the science, substance, and strategies of asset building their initiatives never capture people's imaginations or passions.

Control

As in many situations and relationships, there are people involved with asset building who will attempt to monitor or approve all asset-building efforts in the community.

There are also those who would prefer to give people the information about assets and then send them on their way without the continued contact or guidance necessary to sustain asset-building efforts.

Leadership

Youth are given total responsibility for an asset-building initiative.

Youth are relegated to token roles in an asset-building initiative.

Scope

In order to show results, some initiatives focus so narrowly on one or two issues or actions that they have little broad impact.

Others fall into the trap of creating such a wide range of activities and priorities that documenting or even noticing progress is extremely difficult.

Inclusion

Believing that every group in the community must be represented before action can be taken will do nothing but slow you down.

It's important to also avoid the other extreme of presuming the people who show up are all that's needed and additional outreach is unnecessary.

Programs

Some initiatives take a program-only approach, relying on programs to accomplish all of a community's asset-building goals.

Other initiatives fail to recognize that programs do have their place and exclude them altogether.

Funding

You could spend most of your time and energy searching for and securing funding.

You could ignore the need to find funding for coordination, communication, and technical assistance.

ise is much more considerate, flattering, and appealing than simply saying you need volunteers for a new project and wonder if they'd be interested.

Even if you staff all positions with volunteers, make sure you provide clear, realistic, written expectations and guidelines. Include length of desired commitment, frequency and length of meetings and other activities, and responsibilities.

Adults, Stay True to Your Asset-Building Word

Several years ago, Project Cornerstone, an asset-building collaborative in Santa Clara County, California, was looking to engage young leaders. One person they turned to was 17-year-old Nam Nguyen. Says Nguyen, now a junior at San Jose State University,

> I was already involved in asset building, but didn't use the language. I was out in the community doing prevention work for dating and domestic violence. The asset-building movement in Santa Clara was brand new. Project Cornerstone was looking for young people to come on board. It was interesting—a great idea and pretty fresh—but it was also kind of scary because it was one more thing being introduced. It was brand new and didn't have credibility yet. I decided to give it a shot because of the way the adult leaders supported and empowered me. It was a different experience . . . as soon as I sat down with the steering committee I was one of them. For the first time I felt like I was on the same page and level with adults. The consistency of that feeling is what kept me involved. The adults were true to their word.

When You Go

The leadership qualities needed for an asset-building initiative are somewhat unique in that the work is often amorphous, change takes time, and priorities among the wider community ebb and flow depending on the political climate and other factors beyond your control. The following traits are good to keep in mind as you establish your leadership group.

Attitudes and commitments to seek or cultivate:

➤ Being comfortable with uncertainty, change, and negotiation;

➤ Belief in and ability to empower self and others;

➤ Trust in people, the process, and the community; and

➤ Blended personal commitments and professional action.

Competencies and character traits to build into the leadership groups (recognizing that no one person brings everything):

➤ A mix of strategic and operational thinkers;

➤ People of different ages, and personal and professional backgrounds; and

➤ A balance of people who bring passion (heart) and analytical skills (head).

Connections, credibility, and influence in the community, including:

➤ Positional leaders (heads of major organizations or systems, political or appointed public figures, and so on);

➤ Young people who bring energy and enthusiasm as well as authentic youth perspectives and engagement; and

➤ Individuals with credibility, trust, and relationships that touch all aspects of community life, including groups that typically do not feel welcomed or included.

There are also ways you can model and practice asset building as a group. For example:

Support

1. Take time at each meeting to connect with one another. Supply name tags, and begin with some kind of warm-up that helps people get centered and focused.

2. Make communication a top priority by ensuring that you have accurate contact information for all members (e-mail, phone numbers, mailing addresses) and that everyone receives the same information regarding events, meetings, and other project details.

Empowerment

3. Use a system for decision making that invites dialogue and engages each person in the process. Avoid having people "rubber stamp" decisions that have all but officially been made.

4. Focus on what individuals contribute rather than what they represent.

Boundaries and Expectations

5. Together establish clear ground rules about how the group functions and about what's expected of team members.
6. Clarify roles and expectations regarding group processes such as meeting facilitation, note taking, monitoring progress, and so on.

Constructive Use of Time

7. Use your time well. Invite input into agenda planning, send agendas out in advance, and be clear about which actions are required of each item (discussion, decision, etc.).
8. Honor people's other commitments by not over-scheduling meetings in frequency or in length.

Commitment to Learning

9. Provide regular learning opportunities by inviting local experts to speak to your group about topics related to asset building (such as literacy, educational policy, and alcohol and other drug abuse prevention).
10. Encourage team members to do background research on relevant issues and present their findings to the group. If necessary, suggest resources that will help get them started.

Positive Values

11. Articulate and document the shared values that guide your group's collective efforts.
12. Include ground rules that reinforce honesty, respect, caring, responsibility, and integrity.

Social Competencies

13. Build capacity and skills by rotating leadership and other duties.
14. When new members join, pair them with mentors who can help them learn about how your group functions, get to know other members, and develop the skills they need to fully participate.

Positive Identity

15. Develop a clear sense of your group's purpose and how individuals contribute.
16. Celebrate your shared successes, personal achievements, positive relationships, and vision for the future.

Use the worksheets "Building Your Team" (on page 35) and "Assessing Leadership Skills" (on page 36) to plan, build, and organize your leadership group.

For More Information

An Asset Builder's Guide to Youth Leadership (Search Institute, 1999).

As the Crow Flies

The politics of your community may be more important than size or history when it comes to developing asset-building leadership. There may be professionals or other visible, influential people who can be great champions if included and barriers if left out. And don't let a focus on diversity get in the way of engaging the most enthusiastic of constituents. "Suburban soccer moms," for example, often are viewed as being basically interchangeable. But let us remind you (with apologies to Margaret Mead), "Never doubt that a small group of thoughtful, committed soccer moms can change the world."

Develop Action Plans

Creating an action plan is like taking your map or atlas and drawing in the route you intend to take. Or, depending on the level of organization you prefer, it might be like your travel folder that includes a printed itinerary, contact information, reservation confirmations, tickets, and so on. No matter what form they take, good action plans grow out of visions and goals. They usually include specific information about what will be accomplished when and by whom. They also generally include notes about how each action ties in to the bigger picture of your work.

Building Your Team

To help you think about potential team members or allies, jot down as many names as you can of people you know in each category.

Education: _____

Youth-serving organizations: _____

Neighborhoods: _____

Religious congregations: _____

Youth: _____

Family and social service organizations: _____

Community organizations: _____

Business and industry: _____

Health care: _____

Government: _____

Service clubs: _____

Senior citizens: _____

Juvenile justice and law enforcement: _____

Corporate and philanthropic foundations: _____

Media: _____

Others (higher education, libraries, labor unions, military, realtors, and so on):

_____

Assessing Leadership Skills

Authors James Kouzes and Barry Posner identify essential commitments of leaders. The chart below is adapted from their work, and invites you to reflect on your own leadership group in these terms.

Commitments of effective leaders	Asset connections	Strong	Needs emphasis
They look for possibilities and potential.	Commitment to learning		
They are open to and initiate trying new things.	High expectations		
They have vision.	Positive view of the future		
They engage others.	Empowerment, Social competencies		
They help people work together.	Empowerment, Social competencies		
They make others stronger.	Support		
They are role models.	Support, Boundaries and expectations, Positive values		
They plan small wins.	Social competencies		
They recognize the power of one.	Empowerment, Positive identity		
They celebrate.	Positive identity		

With something as big as a community-wide asset-building initiative, you run the risk of getting too caught up in one aspect of mobilization. If, say, you're conducting a literacy campaign in the context of nurturing the commitment to learning assets, it's easy to see how some constituents and stakeholders could come to view literacy as the core of what you are doing. Emphasizing literacy is certainly a worthy cause, but you probably don't want it to overtake the larger vision.

For top-down approaches to initiatives, a lot of early planning focuses on building the leadership and structure, as well as creating vision, mission, and goal statements. For grassroots mobilizations, the emphasis is more on what people and organizations can do to build assets.

Having an action plan helps ensure that you stay on track and that people understand and implement activities within the larger context of the Developmental Assets framework.

Embracing Fluidity

Whatever you do, put plans in writing and make sure all stakeholders have updated copies. But also be aware that plans change and that is good. It means that your initiative and your community are evolving and growing. In Seattle, Washington, initiative leaders knew this and printed under the title page of their planning document, "This draft plan is fluid and a living document. We expect it will change to reflect our own learning, the ideas of new partners, and opportunities that arise." The Children First initiative includes a disclaimer on the "history" section of their Web site. It reads, "Note: Children First is a fluid initiative. Some of the things mentioned here live on, others have been modified and yet others are no longer." Being prepared for the fluidity helps your group respond to change as the need arises.

When You Go

Below are some ideas for "going with the flow" in an initiative, offered by Search Institute's Gene Roehlkepartain and members of the St. Louis Park Children First steering committee.

▶ Listen a lot. Find out what people care about. Then unleash people's passions, commitments, and interests for building an asset-rich community, whether or not they are part of a structured strategic plan.

▶ Watch for and embrace creativity and innovation on the edges—outside of existing power systems and institutional structures—which may be pointing the way.

▶ Encourage and celebrate small steps that are moving in the direction of big change.

▶ Give lasting change time to take root, emerge, and grow within individuals, groups, and systems within your community. Don't push too hard. Don't give up.

The best action plans grow out of visions and goals that are already in place. Use one of these worksheets "Developing an Action Plan" (on page 38) or "Individualized Asset-Building Plan" (on page 39) for each of your initiative goals. The second one was developed by asset champion and asset-building trainer Cindy Carlson of Hampton, Virginia. Carlson has worked on the initiative in her own community, and she now trains others around the country. She says that though the worksheet looks simple, communities she works with find it very helpful.

Timelines

Well-done timelines have lots of benefits as part of action plans: they are helpful in planning; they serve as visual reminders of goals, objectives, and accomplishments; they can be used as documentation during evaluation; and developing them is often a fun, creative process.

Most timelines are only tentative projections based on action plans. People tend to overestimate how quickly they can get things done, so timelines are generally viewed as works in progress. It's typical to make many adjustments along the way.

Timelines can be used to track or plan tasks between meetings, from year to year, or for the life cycle of a grant. And for a group with patience, a timeline can also be a work in progress for the life of an initiative, as in the case of the Alaska Initiative for Community Engagement (Alaska ICE). With a fantastic network of political leaders, state and federal agencies, school staff and officials, and everyday heroes in place, a goal of ICE is for Alaska to one day become known as the best place in the nation to raise children and youth. But when former coordina-

Developing an Action Plan

Vision:

Goal:

Action in place that we can build on	Action steps to take	Responsible parties	Start date	Completion date

Individualized Asset-Building Plan

Name of organization or group to target:

Contact person for our involvement with the organization:

What is the fit between Developmental Assets and their mission?

What is their self-interest—what's in it for them?

What asset-building activities are they already doing?

What is our goal for involvement with them this year?

Who/what level in the organization do we want to target?

Does this new partnership mean we want to add someone to our leadership group? Who? What materials do we need to share with them?

Who knows someone who can help us get these folks engaged?

What is the long-term goal for their involvement with/contribution to asset building—what is our "end in mind"?

Tentative long-term strategy for meeting this goal:
    Action steps   Timeline
1.

2.

3.

tor Derek Peterson spoke in 2002 with other asset-building champions, he was quick to remind them that it was too early for his team to measure their success in terms of increased assets. Indeed, ICE's hope is to show evidence of change in Alaska in 15 years. Yes, *years*. That's practically a lifetime by today's funding standards.

Peterson was able, however, to point to other indications that their work was well on its way to becoming part of the culture of Alaska: $18 million (including funds from the American Indian Education Equity Act) secured to support their statewide initiative; approximately $35 million leveraged in order to infuse asset building into every school in Alaska; 11 school districts having measured assets using the *Profiles of Student Life: Attitudes and Behaviors* survey (some of them multiple times); 8 regional conferences; support and buy-in from local media; a published book linking assets to the stories and values of Native Alaskans; and relationships, partnerships, and shared commitments forged. The beauty of a physical timeline is that all of these achievements become concrete milestones of success in a culture that doesn't always value or even recognize the importance of patience.

Working backwards from your goals is usually the best way to develop a realistic timeline. Your self-selected "deadlines" may be based on how long you think it will take to accomplish your goals, related to other events in the community, or tied to funding cycles. Whatever your endpoint, starting there will help you determine what's realistic in terms of what can be accomplished by when.

As the Crow Flies

Some people have a knack for turning time-lines into works of art–visual inspiration for and reminders of efforts. If you have someone in your group with this kind of passion, feel free to encourage it. But don't get hung up on the look of whatever you create. Focus instead on making it clear and easy to understand, and on capturing the depth and breadth of your intended actions.

Asset building is a long-term commitment—years and decades rather than weeks and months. You cannot expect to see dramatic changes in a short period of time. You can, however, include in your time-lines markers of your progress, things like choosing a name, providing asset-based training events, and forming an official leadership team. You can also include things that you've already accomplished as a way of reminding yourselves how far you've come.

Every milestone reached is a reason to celebrate, even if it's just a round of applause. Finding joy and satisfaction in the work helps keep enthusiasm high.

Questions to Consider

Alaska ICE uses these questions to help community workshop participants begin to form vision-based action plans:

► What is our goal? (A goal sets direction, but is never fully achieved. It is not objectively measurable but is more like a direction or a concept—broad and subjective. We'll feel it as we move toward it.)
► What need does our goal address?
► How can we create or intensify people's awareness of this need?
► Who are the people who will be involved in implementing our proposed change?
► How can we involve them meaningfully?
► What are the values cherished by the people of the community that we should address when seeking their support for our initiative?
► Who are the key opinion makers whose approval or endorsement we need?
► How can we involve these key opinion makers meaningfully?
► What small-scale efforts (e.g., pilots, field tests) would show viable ways of achieving our goal?
► How can we assure success for our first effort?
► What skills need to be developed for maintaining the sustained change?
► What feedback procedures would assure periodic evaluation for improvement?
► What kinds of resistance ought we to expect?
► What supportive forces are helping us?
► What concrete actions could we take to overcome resistance?

➤ What concrete actions could we take to use supportive forces?

For More Information

Vision Training Associates, in partnership with Search Institute, offers a highly structured community-wide intergenerational retreat called *Generations Together: Your Vision and Plan for an Asset-Rich Community*. This event is designed to help an asset-building initiative create a community-wide mobilization strategy. Information is available at www.search-institute.org/training/sessions/generations.html.

 # Develop Communication Plans

A communication plan is a written strategy for how to get the word out about your initiative and mobilize people to build assets. Though you can simply communicate as you go without a documented plan, sharing ideas, opportunities, and information about asset building is one of the keys to bringing about real change. People have to *know* about the Developmental Assets framework before they can do anything about it.

The Best Place for Kids

The Kansas Health Foundation (KHF) has a vision of making Kansas "the best place to raise a child." One major component of this effort is a public awareness campaign designed to reach thousands of households through print, radio, and television advertising. In addition, organizers recruited influential community leaders and provided them with sales force development training to help them spread the asset-building message. The training included leadership development and strategies for making the concepts relevant to different audiences.

When You Go

A good rule of thumb for communication planning is the old "Who, What, Where, When, Why, How" formula. Though this is often used as a guide for preparing invitations or press releases, these categories can be applied to any form of communication as described below:

Who—As with planning events and other outreach activities, you'll want to first determine whom you are trying to reach. You can start by identifying all the different populations you are targeting and then get specific in terms of messages and strategies aimed at each group (such as youth, parents, business leaders, educators, religious leaders, seniors, and so on). Once you've named all of the groups you want to reach, you can prioritize among them.

"Who" can also apply to others in the communication business that can make your communication planning easier. Local media may want to play a role. Civic groups and other organizations that publish newsletters can provide inexpensive or free (and often very credible) publicity. Also think about local libraries, businesses that communicate with customers or clients, schools, and community groups. If possible, develop a "contacts" list to keep track of potential communication channels.

 ## As the Crow Flies

The size of a community ought to have a big impact on communication strategies. A small town initiative may be able to effectively raise awareness and spark lots of word-of-mouth learning with one billboard, letters to the editor of the local paper, and fliers distributed through the schools. It's a much different story in a large metro area. These communities may want to target individual segments separately (e.g., reaching parents primarily through schools), or combine different vehicles and messages to reach and engage the greatest number of people.

What—Get clear about the messages. Keep them simple and specific so people will be more likely to understand what you're saying and act accordingly. You can learn a lot about what will work by listening to your audiences and developing communication tools and goals that reflect what you learn from their feedback.

Where—You need to know where to find your audiences. Some initiatives have access to mailing lists and send information to people's homes or e-mail addresses. Others use more public forums such as the sides of buses, billboards, and public service announcements (PSAs).

When—Timing is important. Some communities have had success tying communication about assets to other big or notable public stories. Others have found that avoiding competition with other news works better for them. Keeping the messages coming is key. If people hear about Developmental Assets on a regular and consistent basis, over time the concept will become part of their norm. They'll begin to internalize the ideas—and the language— and that will increase their willingness to learn more and try out some of the ideas you share with them

Why—Be sure to name your hoped-for outcomes: What do you want people to do as a result of your communication plan? Why is this outcome important?

How—The how, of course, is about the medium— the methods you use to get what to whom at where when. The methods you choose will depend on what you decide about all of the above. You can use the simple grid on the worksheet, "Communication Plan" (on page 43) for planning how to communicate with people who are working on your initiative, as well as with people in the community.

Questions to Consider

▶ What information, if any, has already been communicated about Developmental Assets, your initiative, or related topics?

▶ How can you tie your communication plans to your vision, mission, and goal?

▶ What outcomes do you hope for and expect from your communication effort?

▶ Who should be involved in developing your communication plans?

▶ Do you need separate plans for internal and external communication?

For More Information

Get the Word Out: Ready-to-Use Communication Tools and Ideas for Asset Builders Everywhere (Search Institute, 2002).

 # Create an Infrastructure

Infrastructure refers to the leadership, systems, and processes that support the capacity of people, organizations, and networks to build Developmental Assets. It's like the aerial map. Though simply having a recognized infrastructure doesn't ensure success, having a lack of clarity usually makes things more difficult.

Asset building is all about empowering people to take action in whatever ways suit their own personal journeys. Therefore your infrastructure should be designed not to *do* or *control* asset building, but to offer inspiration and support to those who do. The two main purposes of an infrastructure are:

1. To cultivate community readiness, energy, and commitment; and
2. To build community capacity to build Developmental Assets.

The diagram (on page 44) illustrates how this happens. The core functions of an infrastructure, as noted in the box on the lower left of the diagram, are:

▶ *Planning, decision making, and governance* that guide both the maintenance issues of the infrastructure and the mission-based priorities of cultivating community capacity for asset building.

▶ *Access resources* (financial, personnel, skills, etc.) needed to support the core functions and capacity-building efforts in the community.

▶ *Convene, network, and organize* committed leaders who have the passion to spread the word and help make the vision a reality. Create opportunities for these champions to learn from, support, and inspire each other.

▶ *Communicate* broadly to the community to inspire and support engagement by distributing information, making presentations, and tapping the media to raise awareness about asset building and local efforts.

Communication Plan

Who
Who is the audience for this message? Who can help us reach the audience?

What
What message are we trying to communicate?

Where
Where can we reach our audience?

When
When should we communicate this message? How often should we repeat it?

Why
What outcomes do we hope to achieve?

How
Which methods will we use to communicate this message?

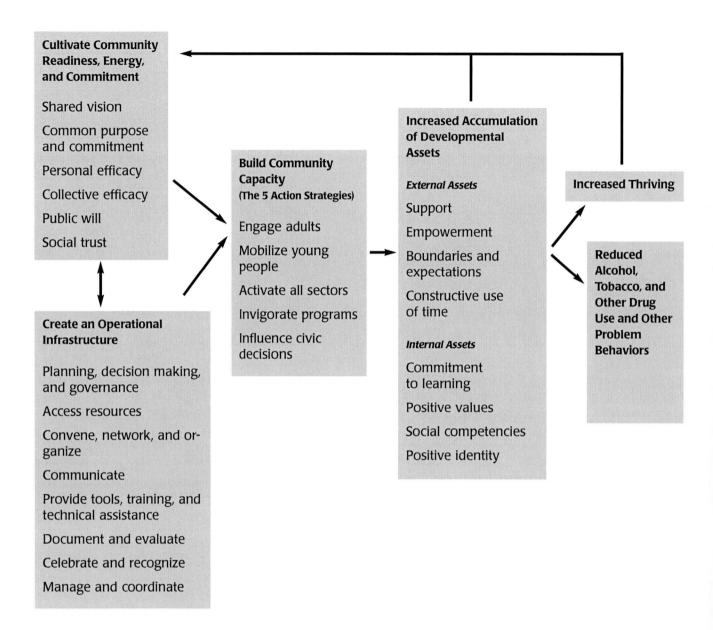

► *Provide tools, training, and technical assistance* that increase capacity of individuals and organizations to engage in, deepen, and sustain their asset-building efforts.

► Initiate and/or coordinate *formal documentation, assessment, and evaluation.*

► *Celebrate and recognize* asset-building efforts and progress in the community.

► *Manage and coordinate* schedules, budgets, and other administrative tasks as needed.

Not a One-Way Street

No single model has emerged as being most effective in supporting and sustaining a community initiative. Each grows out of the realities of the community, the existing resources and networks, political situations, the personalities of initiatives, the interests of funders and other partners, and the kind of journey the community wants to take.

The infrastructure of the Healthy Communities • Healthy Youth Initiative in Orlando, Florida, for example, was based on the premise that community building needs to emerge from the grassroots level. Accordingly, the organizers created what amounts to a technical assistance center, offering information and assistance to local groups seeking to develop asset-building initiatives. In contrast, in Boise, Idaho, five founding agencies (the city government, the YMCA, United Way, a major medical center, and the school district) are each providing staffing and operating support for a strategic plan and formal structure they initiated. And a third model is to hitch asset building to the vehicles of several existing coalitions or groups.

When You Go

Below are ten guiding principles of asset-building initiative infrastructures (regardless of the form they take).

- **Honor the spirit of community**—The energy, enthusiasm, pride, and commitment in a community are much more important to sustaining asset-building efforts than are funding or structure. Nurturing that spirit is essential to effective community building.
- **Engage innovative stakeholders**—Our experience in communities suggests that the best initiators of asset-building efforts in a community are those who not only have a personal and/or professional stake in young people's lives, but who also are likely to adopt and promote new ideas.
- **Form a team of champions**—It is important to start by engaging those who are most enthused and supportive so that all the initial energy is not consumed with trying to engage individuals with different agendas. Among other things, this means that people who are initially engaged need to have a commitment to young people's healthy development and a positive, movement-oriented approach to community building. Once it has stabilized and created some momentum, an initiative will then be ready to build connections with people who do not initially catch the vision. Put another way, a key question is, who can work together?
- **Blend formal systems (top down) and informal networks (bottom up)**—A balance is needed to both engage the formal systems of a community (sectors, institutions, positional leaders) and the grassroots champions (youth and adult). The latter bring energy, creativity, passion, and non-traditional networks into the movement but may not be comfortable with or have patience for the processes and structures that typically guide formal organizational models and collaborations.

- **Emphasize being inclusive and welcoming**—An initiative's structure ought to be such that it invites and is welcoming of *all* people in the community.
- **Plan and do at the same time**—Planning is stepping with the left foot. Doing is stepping with the right foot. Hopping wears people out. Walking can evolve into skipping and eventually running. Integrate your planning and doing so that both planners and doers feel comfortable as part of your effort.
- **Unleash, don't try to control or direct**—As individuals and organizations begin shaping their own approaches and priorities for asset building within the community, it's important that the structure not be designed to control, manage, or direct their efforts. Rather, its role is to build their capacity and give them permission to become actively engaged in asset building within their own sphere of influence.
- **Recognize the importance of "bricks" and "mortar"**—Community building happens best in the informal spaces between traditional structured programmatic efforts. It is like the mortar between the bricks. Unfortunately, organizations are rarely designed to support community building. Community builders are challenged to find ways to support their efforts between the bricks while also building the necessary formal structures.

As the Crow Flies

In a sizable community with sufficient funding, it may be most effective to develop a conceptual infrastructure very early in your initiative. This is particularly true if you are working across city or county lines. In contrast, very small communities may find that enough of an infrastructure of relationships currently exists. In these situations the challenge will be figuring out how to tap into it and maximize the potential of the connections already available.

Planning Our Asset-Building Infrastructure

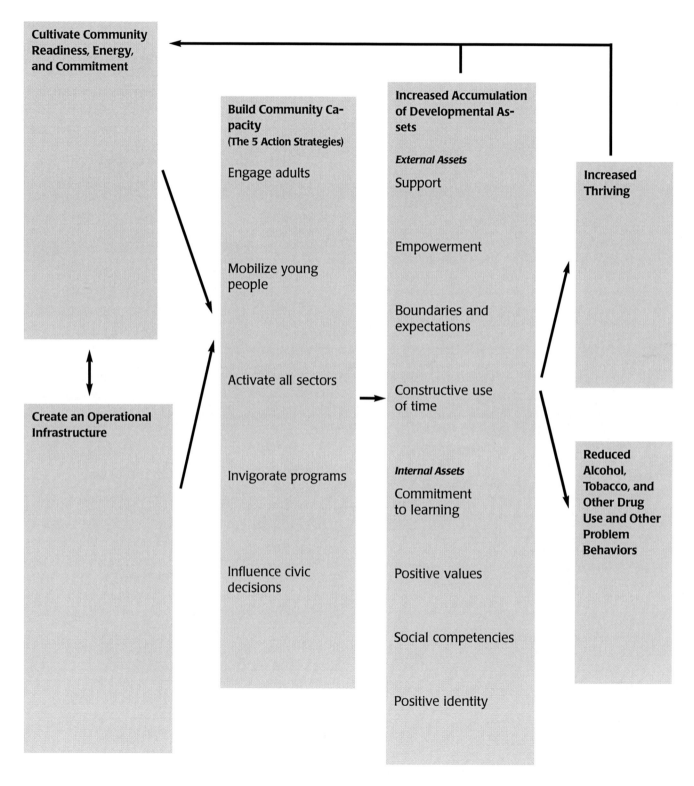

Cultivate Community Readiness, Energy, and Commitment

Create an Operational Infrastructure

Build Community Capacity
(The 5 Action Strategies)

Engage adults

Mobilize young people

Activate all sectors

Invigorate programs

Influence civic decisions

Increased Accumulation of Developmental Assets

External Assets

Support

Empowerment

Boundaries and expectations

Constructive use of time

Internal Assets

Commitment to learning

Positive values

Social competencies

Positive identity

Increased Thriving

Reduced Alcohol, Tobacco, and Other Drug Use and Other Problem Behaviors

➤ **Send a common message through divergent actions**—A careful balancing act is to create enough alignment of message, purpose, and strategy, while also allowing for—even encouraging—individual and organizational innovation, creativity, and self-guided action.

➤ **Accept that this is an emergent, flexible process**—Community building happens in the unpredictable social environment of people. We need to be prepared to let new people come to the table, assume that others will leave, and be open to meetings with emergent agendas. Initiatives stay on track not by sticking to specific agendas, but by continually returning to a shared vision, common values, and agreed-upon operating principles.

Keep your own potential infrastructure in mind as you page through this guide, and note which techniques might be especially useful in your community. For example, Chapter 2 includes a section called "Lead Effective Meetings"; you might find this section useful in cultivating community readiness *or* in building community capacity. The worksheet "Planning Our Asset-Building Infrastructure" (on page 46) offers a blank version of the infrastructure diagram that you can use to help map out your initiative's infrastructure development.

Questions to Consider

➤ What kinds of youth-focused efforts are already underway in your community? How will that impact what you do?

➤ What infrastructures and systems are already in place? How will that affect what you do?

➤ Are there already organizations or collaborations doing (or seeing themselves as doing) the same kind of community-building work? If so, what can you do to connect with them?

➤ Who will be involved in decision making? Who will be responsible for managing finances and other resources?

For More Information

All Kids Are Our Kids: What Communities Must Do to Raise Caring and Responsible Children and Adolescents (San Francisco: Jossey-Bass, 1997).

Assets in Action: A Handbook for Making Communities Better Places to Grow Up (Search Institute, 2003).

Working Shoulder to Shoulder: Stories and Strategies for Adult-Youth Partnerships That Succeed (Search Institute, 2004).

Starting and Supporting Asset Building in Communities (A training offered through Vision Training Associates).

 # Integrate Assets, Prevention, and Other Priorities

It's not unusual for asset champions to find themselves integrating the Developmental Assets framework with other models of positive youth development, community development, or community change, in part because funders sometimes develop preferences for particular models or approaches. Developmental Assets, for example, is recognized and approved as a "Best Practice Prevention Planning Process" by the federal government's Substance Abuse and Mental Health Services Administration's Center for Substance Abuse Prevention (SAMHSA CSAP).

justCommunity Says Just Do It

Some initiatives, such as "justCommunity" in Upper Bucks County, Pennsylvania, have blended frameworks with great success. Lee Rush, executive director of this Healthy Communities • Healthy Youth initiative, wrote in a grant proposal that the Developmental Assets "provide concrete examples of the different protective processes and protective factors." In that same proposal, he presents an approach known as Communities That Care (CTC), a prevention framework based on risk and protective factors. Rush combines CTC with the Developmental Assets framework as pieces of a whole, suggesting both approaches fit well with the five promises described by the national nonprofit organization, America's Promise—The Alliance for Youth. Rush uses CTC risk-factor data to establish the need for action, and he uses a combination of information about protective factors and Developmental Assets to make the case for the positive youth development approach.

Similarly, the Lyon and Storey Counties Healthy Communities • Healthy Youth initiative in Nevada reaches people on "all different levels" with a positive youth development message by tailoring its language and approach to the audience, according to Coordinator Christy McGill. "Among prevention professionals we use Communities That Care," she says, adding that practitioners appreciate the detailed information the model provides. "But to address community-level environmental practices we use [Developmental] Assets. We really think you need both."

When You Go

Like SAMHSA CSAP, government agencies and other funders are increasingly supportive of using the Developmental Assets frame work as a foundation for addressing multiple issues. When shaping an initiative based on blended frameworks or priorities, be able to articulate and present evidence for why you are doing it. There are data available that show the efficacy of asset building when it comes to risk reduction. The asset-building initiative in Oklahoma has published a number of scientific articles demonstrating a reduction in teen pregnancy and other risk behaviors. And the table on page 49 shows clear relationships between the number of assets experienced and a reduction in the likelihood of alcohol, tobacco, or other drug use; mixing alcohol and driving; violence; and other high-risk behaviors. Cite these and other examples you come across as you are gathering information.

Questions to Consider

▶ Why are you blending frameworks or approaches? Will it make your work easier and more productive?

▶ How do your goals tie to each of the frameworks or approaches? Can you show this visually as well as explain it in some detail?

▶ Are there leaders among you who can speak to the power of each framework or approach?

▶ Do your efforts to integrate complicate your efforts to make positive change? If so, is it worth it?

For More Information

Aspy, C. B., Oman, R. F., Vesely, S., McLeroy, K., Harris-Wyatt, V., Rodine, S., & Marshall, L. Adolescent violence: the protective effects of Developmental Assets, *Journal of Counseling and Development*, in press.

Atkins, L., Oman, R. F., Vesely, S., Aspy, C. B., & McLeroy, K. (2002). Adolescent tobacco use: the protective effects of Developmental Assets. *American Journal of Health Promotion*, 16, 198–205.

Kegler, M. C., Rodine, S., McLeroy, K., & Oman, R. F. (1998). Combining quantitative and qualitative techniques in planning and evaluating a community-wide project to prevent adolescent pregnancy. *The International Electronic Journal of Health Education*, 1, 39–48.

Oman, R. F., McLeroy, K., Atkins, L., Vesely, S., Aspy, C. B., Rodine, S., & Marshall, L. (2002). Reliability and validity of the Youth Asset Survey (YAS). *Journal of Adolescent Health*, 31, 247–255.

Create an Initiative Identity

Upon first mention, spending time and energy formulating your identity may seem wasteful. "This is about young people and our community, right?" you may think. "Why does it matter how people perceive our initiative? Why should we invest in that?" But it can matter a

As the Crow Flies

Many people who work in alcohol, tobacco, and other drug (ATOD) abuse prevention, particularly school-based prevention specialists, have been pioneers in the asset-building movement. Long before funders and government agencies got on board, these folks saw the power of Developmental Assets to protect as well as promote health. If you haven't already, learn who the prevention professionals are in your community and make a point of connecting with them and sharing ideas, experience, and enthusiasm.

Patterns of Developmental Assets and High-Risk Behavior among Adolescents

Risk Behavior Pattern	Definition	Number of Developmental Assets (in %)			
		0–10	11–20	21–30	31–40
Alcohol	Has used alcohol three or more times in the past month or got drunk once or more in the last two weeks.	49	27	11	3
Tobacco	Smokes one or more cigarettes every day or uses chewing tobacco frequently.	31	14	4	1
Illicit drugs	Used illicit drugs three or more times in the last 12 months.	39	18	6	1
Sexual intercourse	Has had sexual intercourse three or more times in lifetime.	32	21	11	3
Depression/suicide	Is frequently depressed and/or has attempted suicide.	42	27	14	5
Antisocial behavior	Has been involved in three or more incidents of shoplifting, trouble with the police, or vandalism in the past year.	48	22	7	2
Violence	Has engaged in three or more acts of fighting, hitting, injuring a person, carrying or using a weapon, or threatening physical harm in the last 12 months.	61	38	19	7
School problems	Has skipped school two or more days in the last four weeks and/or has below a C average.	45	24	11	4
Driving and alcohol	Has driven after drinking or ridden with a drinking driver three or more times in the last 12 months.	35	19	9	3
Gambling	Has gambled three or more times in the last 12 months.	30	19	11	4

Source: *Search Institute's aggregate dataset of 6th to 12th grade students in public and/or alternative schools who completed the institute's* Profiles of Student Life: Attitudes and Behaviors *survey during the 1999–2000 school year; N = 217,277 students in 318 U.S. communities.*

great deal. And it is worth the effort to be intentional and thoughtful, because impressions people have of your initiative will influence how they view asset building.

Tying It Together

When the Robbinsdale (Minnesota) Area School District was developing a youth center, staff members knew they had to be strategic about how it was positioned. The plan was for an "integrated services" approach, with many different organizations and groups housed in one building. They also knew that they didn't want the name they chose to be associated just with the building itself, because many of the activities would take place out in the community. In addition, they wanted to be perceived as complementing existing coalitions, including Community Ahead, an asset-building initiative. The youth and adult members of the board of directors brainstormed and evaluated possibilities over a period of several meetings and eventually landed on the name *Mosaic Youth Center* to convey the idea of many complete images creating a larger picture.

When You Go

Even in the information gathering stage, it's imperative to talk about and plan how to manage image and identity. Every initiative will benefit from thoughtful consideration of how it wants to be perceived in the community and by potential partners, funders, and asset builders. Is it important that people know about the initiative itself? Is it enough to simply have them be aware of assets? Do you want the initiative to be seen as linked with or part of another effort or framework? Is it important to have people think of asset building and/or your initiative as something new?

Part of the issue is simply deciding how *you* see yourselves. Your own sense of who and what you are will come through in your conversations, written materials, and other communication. To help guide you, see the "Questions to Consider" on page 51.

Another way to start is by simply creating a name. Some initiatives also help define their identity by developing a logo for stationery, clothing, resource materials, and other strategic locations like billboards, bus stops, and banners at special events. Search Institute has a logo that registered initiatives can modify and use as their own, creating a visual link to national asset-building efforts. Many communities choose to design their own logos, usually incorporating the name they have chosen. What's important is that you create an image that sticks in people's minds and reinforces what you are working toward.

Naming

GivEm 40 24.7 (Traverse Bay area, Michigan)
Take the Time (Multnoma County, Portland, Oregon)
Children First (St. Louis Park, Minnesota)
Raising Arkansas Youth (RAY)

A good name can lend credibility and sustainability to your efforts. People begin to recognize connections where they didn't before if, for example, they hear the name at a school event, read about it in the local paper in reference to a policy meeting, and see it displayed in a community center. Even if people haven't caught on to the idea of asset building, a name gives them a way of talking about what's happening for young people in the community.

Begin your selection process by identifying the criteria for what you want to accomplish. For example, consider whether you want the name to be unique, whether you want to use words like *kids* or *young people,* and if you want to include the name of your community. Typically, the most effective names for asset-building initiatives are short, positive, easy to remember and say, and inclusive of young people birth to age 20. You may want to identify other names in the community with which you would like to be associated or with which you want to avoid competing or overlapping.

At some point after establishing the criteria, plan an intergenerational brainstorming session. Let people be creative and inspired—without comment or critique. It's very important when doing this kind of work to have clear rules about refraining from judgment. People will hold back if they think their idea might be shot down, or even modified.

Once you have a list of possibilities you can engage in some sort of filtering process. Some communities give each leadership team member a number of stars and let each assign stars to her or his top three or five choices. Others ask for one vote from each person. Regardless of the way you winnow down the list, compare contenders with your criteria to ensure that all are met.

When you have a final option or set of options, run it past constituents. Ask them for their honest opinions without giving them yours. You want to hear what people really think, not what they think you want them to say.

Finally, do a trademark search. You'll probably need a lawyer to help you with this. If you've chosen a name that has already been trademarked, you could find yourselves with sticky legal troubles.

Logos

Logos come about in many different ways. Some initiatives customize the HC • HY logo shown here. Others invite young people to submit art for con-

 sideration. Others use a group process to decide on images and then commission one or two artists to work on designs. Still others hire professionals to develop and propose several different options from which to choose.

However you go about it, you'll want to make sure that the logo is simple and gets the message across. Elaborate designs may look great in their original forms, but shrunk down and copied on envelopes, business cards, and other places, they could seem busy and crowded, and the message unclear.

Because logo creation can quickly degenerate into personal preferences, it's wise to begin by identifying criteria for what the logo should and should not do. It should communicate easily and quickly, work well in black and white, and have broad appeal. If possible, bring your designer or designers on board early. Include them in the brainstorming about the criteria as well as possible images.

Once you have two or three designs your group thinks might work, informally run them by constituents to see how people react. When doing this, do not give any explanations or tell them your preferences. You want their first, honest opinions. To ensure useful feedback you can ask questions such as "What's the first thing that comes to mind when you see this logo? What does it say about our community? Have you seen other logos similar to this?"

Once you have selected a final design, develop guidelines about how it can be used. Is it for your group only? If others can use it, are there specifics

about how they get approval, what colors they use, or where they use it? If you are making it widely available it's helpful to have camera-ready copies that others can borrow or have.

Questions to Consider

► What images and ideas do you want people to associate with your initiative?

► What do you hope to accomplish with your name?

► What words, phrases, or images have power in your community?

► What words, phrases, or images would be wise to avoid for political, social, or historical reasons?

► Does your initiative need a unique name or would using the Healthy Communities • Healthy Youth name work? Why?

► Do you want or need to create a logo? Why?

 As the Crow Flies

Creating an identity may be more important in larger communities than in smaller ones. It has been our experience that many times people closest to an initiative, particularly young people, identify more closely with the people involved or the primary location than with the name of the group. A young person involved in a leadership team may tell her friends, for example, that she is going to "Melissa's group" after school, or to the "Y" for a meeting on Saturday morning. An adult may simply be able to refer to the asset-building coalition and people will know immediately what he means. In larger communities it is, for obvious reason, difficult to create this sense of intimacy very deep into the community and therefore a more intentional identity-creation effort may be helpful.

▶ What should your logo reflect about your group or your community?

▶ Are there other logos in your community that are widely recognized? How will that impact what you develop?

▶ What colors will you use? What kind of tone do you want the color to reflect?

▶ Could the designs you're considering have any unintended meanings?

▶ Will the logos you are considering work in different sizes and applications, such as on a banner, a business card, a T-shirt, and letterhead?

▶ Are there local advertising or marketing experts who might be willing to provide pro bono assistance with shaping your image and identity, naming your effort, or developing a logo?

For More Information

Get the Word Out: Ready-to-Use Communication Tools and Ideas for Asset Builders Everywhere (Search Institute, 2002).
For information about using the Healthy Communities • Healthy Youth logo, contact Search Institute at 800-888-7828.

Manage Finances

Money can help, but you don't necessarily need a lot of it. Some initiatives rely heavily on volunteer labor and donated services. Others have comparatively large program budgets, full-time staff, and other "luxuries." Whether you are among the *haves* or the *have nots,* manage your resources well, or you'll quickly become a *have not* in more ways than one.

Some initiatives eventually form independent 501(c)3 nonprofit organizations. Others work under the umbrella of a fiscal agent. Most find that they need to fund at least one paid coordinator to maintain momentum and continuity. Whatever your financial situation you'll want to identify how much funding you want, need, or have. Then you'll need a budget to track revenues and expenses. Your process doesn't need to be complicated or sophisticated, but it does need to be accurate.

We're Not in It for the Money

Can you imagine what you would do if you were part of an all-volunteer asset-building initiative working in a small, economically distressed community and the new CEO of the local hospital came to you with a fantastic fund-raising idea? Give him a hug? Shout for joy?

Surprisingly, if you were part of the Warren County (Pennsylvania) Healthy Community • Healthy Youth Initiative you'd tell him, "Thanks, but we don't raise funds, we build assets."

Hospital administrator John Papalia suggested that Warren County follow the footsteps of many other cities and offer citizens the opportunity to create public works of art intended to generate income and increase tourism. Programs such as the international Cows on Parade auction off the pieces and donate portions of the money to local charities and the arts. They also heavily promote the sculptures to draw visitors and media attention. Papalia thought the initiative ought to develop a local version. And his son happens to be a world-class archer who has connections to a company that makes archery targets and taxidermy forms, including life-size bears that they would sell at a reduced price.

The committee liked the idea, but really didn't have a reason to raise money. "Our whole reason for being is giving asset building away" rather than developing programs or making grants, says Initiative Coordinator Sue Collins. The seed was planted, though, and soon the group came up with the idea of "selling" 50 five-foot bears for the price of one asset-building plan per animal. In other words, anyone or any group could submit a proposal for starting or increasing their asset-building efforts. In exchange, they would receive one fiberglass bear to decorate and display. The guidelines for proposals included a requirement that youth and adult artists work together to create the design. Completed bears are displayed in areas that are accessible to the public.

The bears project is not something the group would have initiated on its own, Collins says.

> This is too much project for us. But we've been able to build connections and develop partnerships that otherwise never would have happened. We [asset champions] have to go where people are. Now we're inviting them to have the *bears*

come to where they are. It draws people into businesses and helps us promote the asset message. This is a win-win-win-win situation for our community and our youth.

When You Go

You can take one of a number of different approaches to financing. You could, for example, create a proposed budget and then look for funding to support it. Or, you could see what funding is out there and available and then create a budget once you know what you're working with.

Budgets

For many nonprofit groups and organizations, the term *budgets* carries negative baggage. In their simplest form, though, budgets are just tools for tracking revenues and expenses. Ideally the budget balances out at the end of the month, year, or other designated point, although that can admittedly be a challenging task. But in and of itself, a budget is not a bad thing: it's a resource that can help you manage your other resources.

Your initiative's need for a budget will depend on your tax status, structure, relationships to other organizations, and funder requirements. Even if you are entirely volunteer run and receive no grants, you'll want a budget that helps keep your finances in order. If you do receive funding you'll have the added motivation of fulfilling your accountability reporting requirements.

Line items are the individual areas of spending within the overall picture of your finances. Many initiatives include in their line items such costs as mailings, printing, photocopying, telephone, fax, and Internet access. Those with paid staff also have to include payroll.

Funding

Financial support for community initiatives can come from a variety of places. Local, county, state, and federal governments are common sources, as are private foundations, fund-raising activities, and contributions from local business. Asking your key leadership team members about funding is often the best way to start. Some of them may have experience in this area or know people in the community who could help you. It's best when at least one member of your leadership group has experience raising funds, because while it doesn't have to be difficult, it takes a certain amount of savvy and persistence. Also keep in mind that some young people, while they may lack experience, can be quite resourceful and effective at raising funds. And organizations may be more apt to fund a proposal when one or more of the writers are young people.

When you approach potential funders, you'll want to have at least a rough draft of a long-range plan that you can share with them to let them know how their contribution will support children and youth in your community. Here are some specific suggestions related to different funding sources:

Local businesses—Some asset-building initiatives recommend asking major employers in your community for grants. Many companies set aside an annual budget for grant making. A company's community relations manager, if it has one, is likely to be your best initial contact. If businesses aren't able or willing to give financial support (or even if they are) they may make in-kind donations such as office space, equipment, services, or supplies. These kinds of contributions can save you a lot of money and

As the Crow Flies

Asset-building initiatives don't always connect directly with Search Institute. In fact, part of the beauty of the Developmental Assets framework is that it can be infused in many different settings in many different ways. We find, though, that when we're not working together—when communities move ahead without the support of Search Institute's network and when Search Institute develops resources and services without consultation with communities—we all spend a lot of time reinventing the wheel. So we encourage all initiatives to at least check in regularly at our Web site for updated information and ideas about how this work is best done.

make the logistics of managing your campaign much easier.

Business or service clubs—Groups such as Rotary or Lions clubs look for ways to strengthen their communities. Many existing initiatives have developed unique and lasting partnerships with such groups.

Community foundations—A quick search of the Internet or your community's yellow pages can yield great information about foundations in your area.

Private foundations—The Internet is also an effective tool for finding out about national foundations that support youth development, community development, and other asset-related initiatives and programs.

Fund-raising activities—Fund-raising can really be fun. Initiatives have held, among many other events, walks/runs, carnivals, and silent auctions. Sales of food items, plants, raffle tickets, and other items can also work well.

Individuals are also sometimes willing to make contributions simply because they like what you are doing and want to support it. Always acknowledge and express gratitude for *any* resources you receive, whether large or small, financial or in-kind.

One of the challenges in securing support from any of these sources, particularly foundations, is developing proposals or grants that outline what you plan to do and how you plan to do it. A number of asset-building initiatives have had tremendous grant-writing success. Take a look at a sample grant proposal template (on pages 55–58) based on a project Search Institute completed with four rural communities in west-central Minnesota over a three-year period. You can use this as a reference when developing your own proposals. If you would like to explore replicating this model, please contact Search Institute.

Questions to Consider

► What are your funding needs? How will you build your revenue?

► Who might be willing to make financial or in-kind donations?

► What are your budgeting needs? Tracking income and expenses? Reporting to funders or potential funders? Filing tax returns?

► Who can keep track of the budget? What training does he or she have or need?

► What basic line items should you include?

► Will you allow reimbursements for initiative-related purchases or activities? If so, what procedures will you put in place?

For More Information

The Sample Grant Proposal is available online at www.search-institute.org/communities/downloads/

Sample Grant Proposal

Proposal Title
Strengthening the Sustainability of Rural Community Asset-Building Initiatives: A Joint Proposal from the Communities of:

- X
- Y
- Z

Project Overview
In times of scarce resources, broad-based community initiatives that focus on building assets for and with their young people face a triple challenge:

(Pick three—or pick two and add one specific to your setting.)

- Their work spans multiple sectors of the community, so no single sector "owns" or funds the work.
- They typically focus on mobilizing and engaging all adults and youth across the community in countless acts of asset building, so they are not viewed as a group of professionals with an easy-to-see agenda.
- They often do not focus on running programs, although they may encourage the infusion of asset building into existing programs and identify gaps in community infrastructure as part of their work.
- Because they are not "a program," they face challenges when trying to measure the progress they are making.

In fact, the more effective they are in infusing asset building throughout existing networks, programs, and systems in their communities, and encouraging everyone to "own" the idea of being responsible for the well-being of their young people, the more invisible the role of the initiative can become.

When this is coupled with the current scarcity of resources in general, and in rural communities in particular, sustainability becomes a very real challenge.

This project has grown out of the willingness of three asset-building community initiatives to collaborate in order to hold down costs and maximize learning and knowledge diffusion across our communities as we take the next step on our journey toward stronger communities and healthier young people.

Background Information
(Select all or some of the following, based on funder's familiarity with Search Institute, the Developmental Assets, and your initiative.)

The framework of Developmental Assets and research on their powerful impact on youth was first released by Search Institute in 1989 in the publication *The Troubled Journey: A Portrait of 6th through 12th Grade Youth.* That same year, Search Institute began to focus planning efforts around the concepts of positive youth development and the creation of healthy communities for children and adolescents. It presented research findings in refereed journals and at conferences across the United States.

On one level, the 40 Developmental Assets represent everyday wisdom about positive experiences and opportunities for young people. Search Institute's research indicates that these assets powerfully influence adolescent behavior—both by protecting young people from risky, problem behaviors and by promoting positive attitudes and choices. This power reaches across all cultural and socioeconomic groups of youth, and additional research suggests that assets have similar implications for younger children.

Unfortunately many young people experience too few of these important building blocks. Surveys of more than 200,000 students in grades 6 through 12 in the 1999–2000 school year reveal that young people experience only an average of 19.3 of the 40 assets. Overall, 56 percent of young people surveyed experience 20 or fewer of the assets. In short, our research shows that young people from all walks of life have too few assets.

Ongoing research from Search Institute and by others continues to increase our understanding of the role Developmental Assets plays in the lives of youth.

(Web pages you can include in the appendix and reference as needed):

What are Developmental Assets?
- www.search-institute.org/assets/

Importance of assets in young people's lives:
- www.search-institute.org/assets/importance.html

Asset lists:
- www.search-institute.org/assets/assetlists.html

Links to research on the Developmental Assets:
- www.search-institute.org/research/assets/

The linkages between assets and academic achievement and linkages between assets and race:
- www.search-institute.org/research/Insights/

Grading Grown-ups: A national study of adult attitudes and behaviors:
- www.search-institute.org/norms/

In 1992, the first community group approached Search Institute to explore how it could create a community that would be intentional about delivering Developmental Assets. Group members recognized that too few youth had enough of these Developmental Assets in their lives and too few adults felt responsible for and knew how they could support the youth of their community.

Since that time, nearly 600 communities in 44 states and several Canadian provinces have started similar asset-building initiatives to guide broad diffusion of an understanding of the importance of Developmental Assets in the lives of youth. These initiatives exist in urban neighborhoods, suburbs, counties, school catchments, and rural communities. While their geography varies widely, they share three characteristics:

- They use the framework of Developmental Assets as a focus for their work;
- They are made up of representatives from at least three sectors of the community; and
- Youth are active partners in the work of the initiative.

A newer body of research relates to how community initiatives can play a strategic part in creating a community-wide consensus about the roles all adults and young people have in this work, and in developing opportunities for sectors and organizations to infuse their work with an asset-building approach.

Search Institute identifies five action strategies that asset-building initiatives undertake:

- **Engage adults** from all walks of life to develop sustained, strength-building relationships with children and adolescents, both within families and in neighborhoods.
- **Mobilize young people** to use their power as asset builders and change agents.
- **Activate sectors** of the community—such as schools, congregations, youth, businesses, human services, and health care organizations—to create an asset-building culture and to contribute fully to young people's healthy development.
- **Invigorate programs**—expanding and enhancing programs to become more asset rich and to be available to and accessed by all children and youth.
- **Influence civic decisions** by working with decision makers and opinion leaders to leverage financial, media, and policy resources in support of this positive transformation of communities and society.

(You may choose to include examples of your initiative successes in any of these five areas to illustrate work done to date.)

Project Detail
Goals and Objectives

(May include any but probably not all of the following):
- Engage in a self-study process to assess progress to date and identify new opportunities to expand the work and strengthen local initiatives.
- Build deeper expertise in local initiatives.
- Connect regularly with Search Institute resources and expertise.
- Host Training of Trainers, as appropriate.
- Mobilize and equip new sectors in three local communities, in order to broaden shared ownership of the work and expand capacity.
  - Connect
  - Train
  - Identify subsequent activities and opportunities within and between communities.
- Engage youth at a deeper level—or engage a larger number of youth.
  - Youth adult training
  - New strategies for engagement
- Deepen focus on intentional work.
- Evaluate progress toward goals.
- Celebrate successes.

Target Audience
While each of our initiatives is trying to reach everyone in our community, for the purposes of this grant each of us will identify sub-audiences we are trying to reach through this three-year process, and will identify target outcomes for those groups.

Methods
The project will begin with a day spent listening deeply to representatives from each community to hear the perceptions, wisdom, and strengths that each community possesses. This is also an opportunity to discuss the challenges that each community faces in becoming more intentional in the shared task of raising youth and the work the community has already accomplished to date.

From the synthesis of data across all communities involved, the initiative coordinators, in conversation with staff from Search Institute, will identify shared needs and opportunities to take their community building work further and develop a three-year work plan. Search Institute staff will draw on knowledge of the nearly 600 communities engaged in this kind of effort, to maximize the information that can infuse the work plan.

The work plan will include steps each individual initiative will be taking, as well as any joint trainings and projects identified that will enhance the work of all the initiatives. One primary goal will be to identify new sectors or organizations that can be brought into the work or existing partners that can be trained to go deeper with their asset-building efforts.

Each initiative will have a small resource account with which to purchase Search Institute materials that will help with its work.

Search Institute staff will visit the communities twice each year. Search Institute staff will manage a linking function using e-mail and conference calls once a month to provide ongoing technical support. Search Institute will provide feedback on and synthesis of each monthly meeting.

Initiatives will each send four representatives (two youth and two adults) to the national Healthy Communities • Healthy Youth conference at least once during this three-year grant.

(Add any other specific agendas that your initiatives have agreed upon in entering into this joint process.)

Staff/Administration
Eight hours of staff time per month will be committed by each initiative to participation in this project, including time to recruit target audiences for trainings and gather key players for meetings and for the HC • HY conference. Ten hours per month of Search Institute staff time will be purchased to provide technical assistance and consultation by phone, by e-mail, and in person to support this project.

Available Resources
- Each initiative agrees to provide staff time to this project at no cost.
- Meeting space?

Needed Resources and Personnel
- Resource account for each community to use to purchase resources from Search Institute.
- Meeting space that will accommodate joint trainings (one per year).
- Trainings from Vision Training Associates and trainer expenses (one per year).
- Ten hours per month of Search Institute staff time.

Needed Facilities
(Determine whether someone in the participating communities has access to meeting space at no cost—if so, include under "available resources"; if not, include meeting room rental here.)

Needed Equipment/Supplies/Communications
- Cost per participant for meals/refreshments for any all-day trainings included. *(Contact Search Institute for assistance in estimating attendance to generate this number.)*
- Flip charts and a screen for trainings. *(Include under "available resources" if you have these available. Trainers/SI typically can provide a computer and multimedia projector for trainings. Other training materials are built into the training fee.)*
- Postage for two or three mailings per year. Most communication between sites and Search Institute will be through e-mail.
- Funding for six conference calls between the three coordinators and Search Institute staff each year.
- Mileage/travel expenses for two visits per year by Search Institute staff person.
- Hotel costs for Search Institute staff person (three nights for the deep listening sessions in each community plus one night for each of the remaining five visits over the three-year period, assuming arrival the day before an event and availability of a flight out the night of the event.)

Budget
For sample budget, contact Search Institute.

Appendices
Timeline
Year 1
- Phone conference call and e-mails between Search Institute and sites to establish working relationship, agree on dates for events, and prepare Search Institute staff for first visit.
- Deep listening sessions *(one day in each participating community).*
- E-mails and conference call to debrief the listening sessions and begin identifying target audiences and tasks—including evaluation strategies.
- Collect baseline data if needed.
- Generations Connected training or small on-site planning session depending on emerging needs.
- Updating by e-mail and bimonthly conference calls.
- Targeted work in each community.

Year 2
- Schedule a training *(include any trainings that you have already agreed upon).*
- Continue bimonthly conference calls and e-mail communication.
- Two visits by Search Institute staff (one may coincide with training).
- Meetings and work will continue in each community.

- Review/carry out any evaluation steps identified in the plan.

Year 3
- Schedule a training *(include any trainings that you have already agreed upon).*
- Continue monthly conference calls and e-mail communication.
- Two visits by Search Institute staff (one may coincide with training).
- Meetings and work will continue in each community.
- Complete evaluation of project.
- Complete final report to funder.
- Celebrate successes.

Letters of Support and/or Cooperation
(These should come from the participating initiatives and Search Institute.)

Evaluation Plan
(To be developed in conjunction with the work plan and taking into account funder requirements. Depending on its complexity, this might require additional funding, or might be something each initiative could carry out on its own.)

Chapter 2

People to See, Places to Go, Things to Do

This chapter provides ideas, suggestions, and tools for mobilizing organizations, systems, and people of all ages to implement the five action strategies for asset-building initiatives.

 **Don't Miss It**

Mobilize Young People and Engage Adults

➤ Mobilize Young People
➤ Engage Adults
➤ Be Inclusive
➤ Lead Effective Meetings
➤ Build Networks
➤ Recruit and Organize Volunteers
➤ Recruit and Organize Staff
➤ Reach Out
➤ Celebrate

Activate Sectors and Invigorate Programs

➤ Activate Sectors and Invigorate Programs

Influence Civic Decisions

➤ Influence Civic Dialogue and Decisions
➤ Plan and Facilitate Events

 **Optional Side Trips**

Mobilize Young People and Engage Adults

➤ Create a Speakers Bureau
➤ Host a Link 'n' Learn
➤ Train Asset Builders
➤ Use the Internet
➤ Form Task Forces

Activate Sectors and Invigorate Programs

➤ Form Partnerships
➤ Pass Resolutions

Influence Civic Decisions

➤ Hold Town Meetings
➤ Release Survey Results

Mobilize Young People

If you believe that youth vote with their feet, you probably have a pretty good sense of how well you're already doing when it comes to creating a youth-friendly environment within your initiative. The common belief is that if young people care about or enjoy something enough, they'll get involved. Of course, they also have to know about it.

In very rare cases young people are part of the core group in a community that initially gets excited about asset building. More often, though, adults have the idea and then want to bring young people into the mix. When this happens there are two major questions to address: "What are the best ways to let young people know about our efforts?" and "What can we do to get and keep them engaged?"

Even "Off-the-Wall" Youth Can Build Assets

Making personal contacts and looking beyond the natural leaders are two keys to successfully engaging young people. For example, Luke Johnson of St. Louis Park, Minnesota, says that when he was in junior high someone who already knew him and his mom recruited him for the Children First vision team. Aside from the woman who asked him to be involved, most people didn't think he cared about making a difference in his community, he reports.

> I wasn't a super troublemaker, but I was mischievous. I got in trouble for talking a lot. My friends . . . thought of me as a goofball. It isn't that they looked at me as a bad person, just kind of off-the-wall.

Five years later Johnson was the team's co-chair and a strong believer in the power of assets.

> When I first started going to the meetings I didn't comprehend the whole idea. I just knew that they wanted to make a difference for kids. I thought it was cool that adults listened to me and wanted to hear what I had to say.

And says Johnson, he was pleased to be included in something alongside youth in high school.

Now Johnson's understanding of the Developmental Assets has grown and he sees them as a tool for helping people realize "the ultimate goal" for what young people can be if they have the right supports and opportunities. He says that the assets are:

> the things that an ideal youth has . . . not in the sense of being an all-star basketball player or straight-A student, but in terms of being a helper and role model—someone kids can look up to and adults can be proud of.

When You Go

Like Luke Johnson, T. J. Berden of Traverse City, Michigan, has a history with asset building. Berden got involved with GivEm 40 24.7 early in his high school years. He has been a leader in the initiative, including a five-month run as a paid intern. Here's Berden's advice for asset champions hoping to engage young people in their initiatives:

► Don't worry much at first about using the asset language. "It's hard language to get right off the bat." GivEm 40 started out using a teen theater group to develop and perform skits based loosely on the assets so that "we could show what youth could do." Once young people were interested and engaged, the group "then slowly introduced the framework."

► "Put youth at the forefront, make it about them, make it their priority . . . The community needs to hear from youth. It's one thing to have adults say, 'This is about what youth need.' It's much different to have a youth come to the table and say, 'Here's what my life is like, here's what I need.'"

► Diversify your focus and bring young people on board in ways that appeal to them. According to Berden, GivEm 40 started out with about 5 to 10 youth leaders. He got involved through a theater class he was taking that was asked to develop skits on community, family life, and positive affirmation. It came off "really nicely" and the group was encouraged to continue.

But he wouldn't have joined if "they had come to my school and said, 'Hey, we're doing this asset building thing.'" Other youth will have similar responses, he says, unless their interests or needs are met through their involvement.

Now that we're branching off into community—doing [a youth section in the local] newspaper, youth arts forums—youth are getting interested. Now we probably have 40, 50, or 60. I never thought I'd see that. We were always pushing for it but nobody could quite grasp this intangible thing. Now there is something they can hold on to. You need to get them involved in something they are interested in: theater, sports, writing. You can get advocates within those groups.

► If you're looking to recruit young people, contact your local schools, youth-serving organizations, congregations, and neighborhood groups. Ask them if they'd be willing to be involved and to bring some young people with them. Let them know that you're not necessarily looking for students who are already involved in a lot of activities. You want people who care about their communities and who are willing to find out what asset building is about.

Engaging College Students

Engaging college students in asset building is an entirely different issue. In many cases college students are away from home for the first time, making more independent choices about classes and activities, and adjusting to new ways of managing their time and energy.

Here are some thoughts from college students Nam Nguyen and Leah Verhoeven, members of the Project Cornerstone steering team in Santa Clara County, California, on how to get or keep college students involved with your initiative:

Question: A lot of people wonder how to get and keep young people involved in asset building. How did you first connect with Project Cornerstone and the Developmental Assets?

LV: Having been in Girl Scouts my whole life I was involved in asset building in a roundabout way. Girl Scouts is an asset-building organization, but doesn't use the [asset language]. Just after high school graduation I was recruited, through the Girl Scouts, to facilitate daylong Project Cornerstone leadership retreats for middle and high school students. After a while they asked me to be on the steering committee. I've been going to the monthly meetings ever since.

The first time I ever interacted with the steering committee was a summer planning retreat. They said, "Hey, come out. It will be fun." Every time I said something they looked at me, they listened, they took a minute to reflect, and made sure they really understood what I was saying. A lot of adults don't do that. I really felt welcome and appreciated. And they still listen. They ask me questions, seek out my opinion . . . they don't just wait for me to say something.

Question: What role in asset-building initiatives can young adults play that is unique from that of younger youth or older adults?

LV: College students are in between—almost adult, but with youth perspective. High school students can be very mature and have a lot to contribute, but they are generally more in the "youth mode." College-aged youth can be a good link because they can look back on childhood but they're not quite adults yet.

Question: Do you have any advice for initiatives that are trying to get or keep young adults involved?

LV: Be flexible. Some months are really difficult for me to go to meetings. If you have a rigid expectation or schedule, students aren't going to want to be there. Then give them real roles and respect their time and contributions.

NN: In high school you can still relate to having assets built in you. As soon as I reached college I felt like there was this gray area for asset building (and for a lot of things in general). The research is based on a young demographic. I used to see it as a child development tool. As soon as I reached college it was harder for me to see it that way. Asset building is great for everybody. It's a framework for people. Who wouldn't like to have three role models? Who wouldn't like to have supportive neighbors in their dorm that they can really connect with? Peer to peer, everyone to everyone, it's very encompassing for all generations. This needs to be put in perspective for young adults who feel like they are in this gray area.

All kinds of people are asset builders. Although most don't have *all* of the characteristics listed below, all the strengths youth have or develop will help them support and nurture their own development and that of their peers.

You are or could be . . .
► Open and honest.
► An active listener.
► Committed to integrity, responsibility, helping others, and promoting positive change in the world.
► Hopeful and optimistic about the future.
► Self-aware and committed to positive growth.
► Appreciative of others' strengths and uniqueness.
► A caring and supportive friend.
► Reliable and trustworthy.
► Willing to share your time, knowledge, caring, interests, and experience with others.

You already or could begin to . . .
► Greet adults or ask simple questions as a way of taking initiative in building relationships.
► Respect adults and expect respect in return.
► Seek to understand adults.
► Believe in and take good care of yourself.
► Get involved in sports, arts, or other activities that interest you.

► Look for the good in others and seek common ground with them.
► Engage in healthy relationships with adults, peers, and younger children.
► Get to know your friends' parents.
► Talk with people you trust about personal values, beliefs, decisions, and cultural differences.
► Model positive behaviors including kindness, lifelong learning, civic engagement, and self-restraint.
► Forgive mistakes, yet hold people accountable.
► Know how to apologize, explain, negotiate, and resolve conflicts peacefully.
► Work hard to do well in school, serve your community, and be a valuable resource through both your words and your actions.
► Use the asset framework to guide your interactions with others and to check on your own healthy development.

In the workbook *Take It to the Next Level: Making Your Life What You Want It to Be* (Search Institute, 2003), the asset categories are presented in slightly different language thanks, in part, to input from a number of young asset champions. The booklet is designed to help young people go beyond understanding asset development into making it real in their own lives. Here are the categories:

Who really cares? We all need other people—whether to encourage us during tough times or to celebrate with us during good times.

The power to make a difference. When you decide that no matter what happens to you, you're going to make the best of your day, that's having power.

Who's in charge? So what would life be like without rules and expectations? Like driving down a highway with everyone driving different directions to different destinations with no rules.

What do you want to do? One part of who you are is how you spend your time.

Live and learn. We're all born with natural abilities and gifts, even if we don't get to choose which ones we get. What are important are discovering the abilities and gifts each of us does have, trying hard and not giving up, and learning how to handle frustrations and disappointments to keep growing strong.

You "gotta" believe in something. Everyone has values—ideas about people and life that they believe

As the Crow Flies

There is lots of talk these days about how youth are "overprogrammed." And it is certainly true that many young people go from school to after-school programming to weekend events or social engagements. But there is also a segment of the youth population that has little to do beyond school. When looking to recruit young people for your asset-building initiative, keep an eye out for these folks. They have the time and probably more need than those who would see your initiative as just one more thing on an already busy calendar. Better yet, involve "underprogrammed" young people and their parents.

in. Some values can help you live your life well; some values can get in your way. Do you know what your values are?

How do we all just get along? "Getting along" isn't easy for most human beings. Part of what makes it difficult has to do with stereotypes (unproven beliefs, good or bad, about people) and prejudices (judging an individual by the characteristics of a group that individual is a member of, without getting to know that person).

Good to be me. No one is ever done growing and changing—we all do it throughout our lifetimes. If you choose to, you can work at becoming stronger and wiser.

Questions to Consider

Take a look at how you are approaching youth engagement by reflecting on these basic questions about recruiting and orienting young people.

➤ Are you clear about what's needed?

➤ What do you tell people about what your initiative and asset building are all about?

➤ What do you tell young people about what you hope for from them?

➤ Are you creative about how you recruit?

➤ Where do you "look for" young people to be involved?

➤ How are you tapping the resources that are most readily available to you?

➤ How are you reaching out beyond your regular circles?

➤ Do you strive for equality and diversity?

➤ How are you working to be inclusive of people of different backgrounds, views, and interests?

➤ What are you doing to create a welcoming, hospitable environment for all people involved in your initiative?

➤ Do you have an effective orientation for young people?

➤ What do you do to introduce young people to your initiative and the Developmental Asset framework?

➤ How do you welcome young people so they feel empowered and invested in what you are doing?

➤ What else would you like to do to effectively recruit and orient young people to your initiative?

For More Information

Working Shoulder to Shoulder: Stories and Strategies of Youth-Adult Partnerships That Succeed (Search Institute, 2003).

 # Engage Adults

Virtually every major social movement in this nation has begun with individuals making personal commitments to addressing a need or a cause in their own lives, in their community, or in the world. Building young people's foundation of assets is no different. In fact, personal commitments to building relationships with youth are critical to the success of the movement. No matter how much money is spent, how many elaborate programs are initiated, how many laws are passed, or how many professionals are hired, the experiences of young people will not fundamentally change unless individuals—both adults and young people—take personal responsibility for contributing to young people's healthy development.

Other People's Kids

One of the major challenges in mobilizing adults as asset builders with young people outside their own families is that we live in a society that doesn't expect adults to take responsibility for "other people's kids."

In the *Grading Grown-Ups 2002* national telephone survey, Search Institute found that most adults and youth *believe* it is important for adults to connect with children and youth outside their families in many different ways, such as encouraging school success, teaching shared values, and teaching respect for cultural differences. Yet both young people and adults agree that most adults *don't do* these positive activities regularly.

 # When You Go

The *Grading Grown Ups* study revealed some factors that make a difference when it comes to adults engaging with youth. Adults are more likely to be engaged with young people when they experience a strong social expectation to be involved, when they talk with parents and other adults about *how* to be involved, and when they are involved already in their communities. Based in part on this information, you can break down the task of engaging adults into four smaller steps: building awareness, encouraging simple first steps, inspiring action, and making asset building a way of life. You can also regularly remind adults that all kinds of people are asset builders. Although most people don't have *all* of the characteristics listed below, all the strengths adults have or develop help them support and nurture the young people in their lives.

You are or could be . . .
- ► Open and honest.
- ► An active listener.
- ► Committed to integrity, responsibility, helping others, and promoting positive change in the world.
- ► Hopeful and optimistic about young people and the future.
- ► Self-aware and committed to positive growth.
- ► Appreciative of others' strengths and uniqueness.
- ► A caring and supportive friend and colleague.
- ► Reliable and trustworthy.

As the Crow Flies

Adults get into asset building lots of different ways. Whenever possible, tap into the unique interests and priorities of individuals when recruiting adults for asset building. If a business owner does not have an interest in or sense of responsibility for young people, point out the advantages to having a healthier, stronger population of young people who might be present as future customers, clients, or employees. When targeting teachers emphasize that asset building is not "one more thing to do" but a way of thinking and being that enhances the classroom environment. And with parents, focus on the things they already do right and how asset building can help them do even better. No one wants to be told they're doing something wrong.

- ► Willing to share your time, knowledge, caring, experience, and wisdom with young people.

You already do or could begin to . . .
- ► Greet young people or ask simple questions as a way of taking initiative in building relationships.
- ► Respect and affirm youth and children and expect respect in return.
- ► Seek to understand young people.
- ► Believe in and take good care of yourself.
- ► Attend young people's sporting, arts, or other events.
- ► Look for the good in others and seek common ground with them.
- ► Engage in healthy relationships with young people, elders, and peers.
- ► If you are a parent, invite other caring, responsible adults to be part of your children's lives.
- ► Talk with young people about personal values, beliefs, decisions, and cultural differences.
- ► Model positive behaviors including kindness, lifelong learning, civic engagement, and self-restraint.
- ► Forgive mistakes, yet hold people accountable.
- ► Know how to apologize, explain, negotiate, and resolve conflicts peacefully.
- ► Encourage young people to succeed in school, serve their communities, and be valuable resources through your words and actions.

Use the asset framework to guide your interactions with young people and to check on your own healthy development.

Questions to Consider

- ► Who are the adults in your community who are already committed to asset building?
- ► Who are the adults who are trusted by young people and their parents and who could be brought on board with your initiative?
- ► Who are the adults who may not be interested in developing significant relationships with young people but who could play other roles in your initiative?
- ► What are the barriers in your community to young people and adults developing positive relationships? How could you (or do you) address those issues?

For More Information

Everyone's an Asset Builder (Training available from Vision Training Associates).

Taking Asset Building Personally (Search Institute, 1999).

What Kids Need to Succeed: Proven Practical Ways to Raise Good Kids (Free Spirit Publishing, 1998; available from Search Institute).

Be Inclusive

Truly focusing on all young people in a community means being conscious of and intentional about welcoming and reaching out to all people in your community, regardless of real or perceived differences. In most cases it means going beyond making an effort to taking some healthy risks, putting yourselves in unfamiliar or uncomfortable situations, and pushing the boundaries of age, race, culture, religion, socio-economics, abilities, and other things that keep people apart.

In most communities being inclusive is not easy. In some cases it feels impossible. But the more we can bridge the gaps that divide, the better off our young people will be. The Developmental Assets framework can serve as a common ground, a starting place for real, productive conversations about what we want for our children and youth and how we think we can work together to get there.

Honoring Diversity: Making It Real . . . and Personal

The Minnesota Institute of Public Health works with many different groups and organizations to promote healthy choices among all peoples. They've developed the questions on page 66 that can help you examine your beliefs, stereotypes, knowledge, and understandings of different social, cultural, racial, generational, economic, or other type of groups.

When You Go

Whether or not it is openly acknowledged, there is diversity within your community. In some cases, as with race or ability, the differences are generally apparent. Others, such as religion, sexual orientation, or political leanings, are subtler or even hidden.

It's not your job to identify all of the different groups within your community, but you'll have much more success as an asset champion if you do as much as possible to bring many different "types" of people on board early on. If your initiator group is relatively homogeneous, plan to meet early on with leaders of other groups or organizations that serve more diverse audiences and may be able to join you or at least speak well of you among their contacts.

You also will want to find out what specialized media outlets exist in your area. They can offer recruiting suggestions and give your effort credibility and coverage.

To reach out effectively and truly engage a diverse pool of participants also requires walking a fine line between acknowledgement and assumption. By acknowledgement we mean not pretending that bias and dominance don't occur. By assumption we mean (a) taking for granted that everyone who fits a similar description is the same, (b) figuring that having diversity among your group is too difficult to achieve, or (c) believing that one person can represent an entire population or subgroup. Here are some suggestions for how you can find balance between acknowledgment and assumption:

▶ Learn how the assets work among different groups of youth and for different types of adults.

▶ Tie asset building to the culture of your community. In Alaska, for example, initiative leaders tied the Developmental Asset themes to Native Alaskan stories and values, and published them in a book called *Helping Kids Succeed Alaskan Style*. Assets for Colorado Youth (ACY) has identified traditional Spanish-language parables that tie to the asset categories.

▶ Highlight asset building during culturally specific events and celebrations such as Black History Month, Jewish High Holidays, disability awareness campaigns, Lent, Asian New Year, Rainbow Families events, and so on.

Making Diversity Real . . . and Personal

Are my attitudes toward _____ (name of group) people open and welcome?

Am I comfortable around _____?

Am I familiar with terms preferred by _____ that are unbiased and inclusive?

Do I understand the issues that _____ face in the workplace and community?

Am I well versed in the historical background and contributions of _____ to society?

Do I have more than one _____ peer or colleague that I can openly talk to about racial matters?

Do I see more than one _____ person on a social basis, and am I aware of the diversity within this group?

Can I disagree with a _____ person without feeling intimidated or guilty?

Can I openly disagree with a biased comment made in my presence about _____ people?

Am I involved in a community organization that benefits _____ people?

Do I know names of _____ leaders both nationally and locally?

- Whenever you are developing print materials or outreach campaigns, use diversity as a filter. Ask yourself whether your messages or materials reflect biases or assumptions—obvious or subtle—that may alienate or simply not appeal to certain audiences. A simple thing to be aware of is language. Many communities provide the lists of 40 Developmental Assets and other asset-based resources in different languages because they have high populations of English language learners.
- Find out about diversity awareness activities and cultural groups within your community's schools. Look for ways to learn from or partner with them.
- Avoid lumping people into categories with which they don't feel connected to or even comfortable. Make the time and effort to become familiar with the dynamics of different groups in your community. As examples, it may work to address unique issues and concerns of homosexual and transgender people under the "umbrella" of GLBT (Gay, Lesbian, Bisexual, Transgender), while the majority of the population of Spanish-speakers may reject the generic *Hispanic* label.

Questions to Consider

- Why do you want to be inclusive?
- Are there efforts already underway in your community to build bridges among different religious, cultural, socio-economic, or other types of groups? How successful have they been? Is there the possibility of collaboration?
- What strengths do you have in your community that can help you be inclusive? What barriers might make it difficult?
- What can you do to build on strengths and work around, through, or over barriers?

For More Information

Helping Kids Succeed—Alaskan Style (State of Alaska and Association of Alaskan School Boards, 1999).

The Spirit of Culture (Denver: Assets for Colorado Youth).

Assets for Colorado Youth: www.buildassets.org.

Lead Effective Meetings

Meetings are a fact of life for asset-building initiatives. Some people love them, some people loath them, but they are in many cases the most effective, efficient way to get things done. Effective and efficient, that is, when they are well run. In fact, with good leadership and processes in place, meetings can even be fun.

Getting Things Going

When editor Kalisha Davis called for submissions for *Get Things Going: 50 Asset-Building Activities for Workshops, Presentations, and Meetings* (Search Institute, 2000), a number of asset champions jumped at the opportunity. The result is a book that's full of ideas and suggestions for how to infuse energy and enthusiasm into gatherings, proving that getting together to work on issues and concerns can actually be something that people get excited about.

As the Crow Flies

Asset building can be a great neutralizer in a highly polarized society. Because it is focused on *what* young people need to succeed in life and not *how* to help them succeed, people with very different worldviews can agree on the core concepts. The challenge that remains is to keep an open mind about how asset building is done. If you "give it away," as we believe is most powerful, people can approach asset building from their own frames of reference. We encourage you to put aside, as best you can, differences, and watch and learn from the many ways that people put ideas into action. While you may not always agree, there are great lessons to be learned when we keep our minds and hearts open.

When You Go

Planning and facilitating a good meeting is much more art than science, especially when you have youth and adults working together. There are, however, some tried-and-true ways to *bring down* a meeting—allowing one or two people to dominate, not having a clear agenda, starting or ending late, and so on. All of these show a lack of respect for participants. Here are some keys to success:

Getting Started

▶ Be creative and sensitive about meeting times and places. If, for example, evening meeting times interfere with teens' after-school jobs, and weekends raise transportation issues, meet on a weekday during lunch in the school cafeteria.

▶ Eliminate transportation as an obstacle by identifying group members who can offer rides to those who need them.

▶ Learn the needs of participants. If youth come to meetings straight from school they might need a snack. Adults who come to evening meetings may need child care onsite. If the young people in your group don't carry calendars, make reminder calls a day or two before each meeting. (You may need to regularly check in with participants about whether their needs are being met. People may be reluctant to voice concerns if they think they are the only ones who feel a certain way.)

▶ Include a mix of people and don't expect anyone to speak for an entire group.

As the Crow Flies

You'll may not always be able to plan or lead a meeting that pleases everyone. Some like short and to the point. Others value the process and the time spent together as much as any result. When planning your agenda start with identifying what you and others want and need to get out of the gathering. Make some phone calls if you have to, to gather information from other participants.

Communication and Language

Words and the way they are used can be powerful and, at the same time, very subtle. Talk openly about language issues from the start. Will you use first names? Is the term *kids* acceptable? What about statements such as "You're too young to understand" or "You're too old to understand"?

▶ Pay attention to and confront unfair biases. Watch for unconscious stereotyping of people by age, appearance, clothing style, gender, race, economic status, or other "demographic" factors.

▶ Give each participant—youth and adult—opportunities to speak and be heard.

▶ Make an effort to take young people seriously. We live in a culture where that's uncommon, so regardless of how committed you are to asset building it can be a challenge. Be ready to redirect the conversation if adult participants begin to dominate or treat youth disrespectfully.

▶ If young people are hesitant to speak up or tend to respond with "I don't know," help them identify the reasons for their reticence (such as fear of being put down or difficulty knowing when people are done talking). Be affirming when young people do speak up.

Training, Support, and Process

Bring all new people—youth and adult—up to speed when they join a meeting or group. If appropriate, provide a pre-meeting orientation that includes an overview of your goals, process, grounds rules, and so on.

▶ Be aware of the developmental needs of young people and accommodate the preferred learning styles of all group members. This may mean adding more experiential meeting elements, augmenting written and verbal communications with visual aids, and breaking into small groups.

▶ Start each meeting with a short game or other fun activity that helps all participants with the transition from other activities to the meeting.

▶ Plan concrete projects, give youth responsibilities, and expect achievement.

▶ Let young people learn from their own mistakes.

▶ Be clear about each participant's role and level of authority, time commitment, and length of commitment.

Meeting Reaction Form

Thank you for participating in this meeting! To help make our future meetings most useful to you, please circle the number that best describes how you felt by the end of today's meeting _____.
(date)

For the most part I felt

Comfortable	1 2 3 4 5	Uncomfortable, because _____
		_____
		_____
Respected	1 2 3 4 5	Not respected, because _____
		_____
		_____
Involved	1 2 3 4 5	Uninvolved, because _____
		_____
		_____
Informed	1 2 3 4 5	Uninformed, because _____
		_____
		_____
Satisfied	1 2 3 4 5	Dissatisfied, because _____
		_____
		_____
Interested	1 2 3 4 5	Bored, because _____
		_____
		_____

Comments/suggestions:_____

_____

_____

Name (optional): _____

▶ Ask participants to evaluate each meeting on a regular basis (see the sample evaluation form "Meeting Reaction Form" on page 69).

Questions to Consider

▶ Are meeting agendas planned in advance?

▶ Is a printed agenda available at each meeting?

▶ Do participants follow the agenda?

▶ Are minutes from the previous meeting distributed?

▶ Are there designated roles for each meeting such as facilitator, recorder, and timekeeper?

▶ Do meetings start and end on time?

▶ Do people listen to each other?

▶ Is there time built in for relationship building?

▶ Do most invitees attend? Do they actively participate?

▶ Are conflicts handled efficiently and constructively?

▶ Is there a balance between planning and action?

▶ Is progress made between meetings?

▶ Are differences of opinion respected?

▶ Are meetings energizing?

As the Crow Flies

There is no way around it: networking takes time. Some people readily accept and even embrace the process of building relationships and trust. Others want to get to "work" right away. Those people tend to get frustrated by the slowness of networking. They also might be inclined to be happy with existing connections and less likely to ask, "Who else should be involved?" Particularly in larger communities, that question should always be on the table. When it comes to making a positive difference for kids, we always need to be on the lookout for others who share our commitment, compassion, and enthusiasm. Some people are bound to be antsy about networking and others are bound to feel the process is rushed. It's just how it is.

▶ What's one thing you really like about your initiative meetings?

▶ What's one thing you'd like to change about your initiative meetings?

For More Information

Get Things Going: 50 Asset-Building Activities for Workshops, Presentations, and Meetings (Search Institute, 2000).

Build Networks

In many ways an asset-building initiative is really a network-building effort. Asset champions seek to connect with others in their communities who care enough about young people's healthy development to take action. Asset builders seek to connect with young people. Parents find connections with other adults in the community who can support them and their children. And your leadership team is most likely a web of people who represent different sectors, organizations, or stakeholder groups. These networks are all critically important when creating a developmentally attentive environment. Also important are formal, functional networks that your leadership team develops with other groups and organizations that have similar missions, visions, or reasons for being.

Uniting Congregations for Youth Development: Lessons in Networking

Several years ago, Search Institute engaged in a fascinating experience sponsored by the Dewitt Wallace-Reader's Digest Fund. Known as "Uniting Congregations for Youth Development" (UCYD), the project centered on motivating, equipping, and supporting people of all faiths to be intentional about building assets in their own congregations and in the wider community. The four main strategies were speaking engagements, networking, training, and providing resources. While the participants were all from religious congregations, the lessons learned about networking can be transferred to many organizations and environments. The diagram on page 71 shows the key components of successful networks as developed by the UCYD project team.

When You Go

Relationships are not the main purpose of a network, but they must come first in order to lay a solid foundation. Then it's important to organize: develop a vision (however simple and straightforward) for your work together; identify leaders or people with primary responsibility for keeping the network going; and develop a plan. Again, all of this can be simple and straightforward, but it will help ensure that your time spent together is dedicated to build-ing assets rather than regularly revisiting why you're spending time together.

In their book, *Networking Congregations for Asset Building,* Ann Betz and Jolene Roehlkepartain write, "The next three elements are somewhat fluid. They (in any combination) are what give purpose to a net-work and provide a reason for diverse [groups] to work together over time." They suggest that, depend-ing on its vision, the network may choose to focus efforts on:

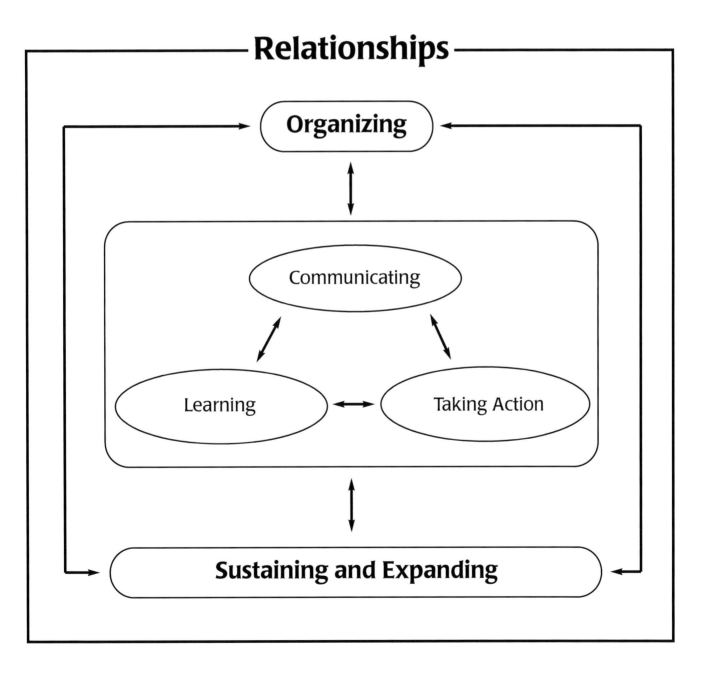

➤ Communicating with others about asset building;
➤ Learning more about asset building; and/or
➤ Taking action individually or together for asset building.

The authors also offer these five steps for getting started:

1. Identify potential leaders (with interest or investment in children or youth development, community development, community change, or community mobilization) whom you know personally. Ask if they are interested in being allied with you as advocates for asset building. Share your ideas and explore their interests. Find out with whom they would be willing to speak about your efforts.

2. Explore the current state of relations between stakeholders before you try to establish a widespread network. Even though some organizations may be on board with your efforts right away, it's possible that there have been conflicts in the past. If there have been major issues (such as competition for funds that turned aggressive or unpleasant), learn as much as you can about them and find out how they have—or have not—been addressed.

3. Host an initial meeting of leaders who have expressed interest. Find out what interests them and do a lot of listening. You may find it helpful to do a brief introduction on asset building to your initiative. Then identify others who should be invited to participate, paying particular attention to being inclusive. Decide who will invite them. Personal connections are usually the most effective for getting people to join something new.

4. Host several discussion meetings. Questions to address might include:
   ➤ Who else should be involved in this effort? How can you make those linkages?
   ➤ What do you want to emphasize? Will this group meet regularly in addition to your regular leadership group meetings? If so, how can you avoid redundancy and make sure everyone gets the information they want and need?
   ➤ How can you all work together to maximize your asset-building potential?

5. Form task forces or other systems to get the work done.

Questions to Consider

➤ Why do you want to build a network beyond the group of asset builders you already have?
➤ With whom and with what groups do you hope to network?
➤ What do you intend to accomplish by building these networks?
➤ What ideas do you have for how you can collaborate with your networks to build assets?

For More Information

Networking Congregations for Asset Building (Search Institute, 2000).

Recruit and Organize Volunteers

For asset-building initiatives, one key to a successful journey is including among the travelers people of all ages who give their time and talent without getting paid. It's important to have many people volunteering to build assets for and with young people, including those who donate their time to work on the initiative itself. These are the people who will most often be able to take good ideas and run with them in the community.

Every Little Connection Matters

The Moorhead (Minnesota) Healthy Community Initiative (MHCI) started with a strong volunteer base because the initiative grew out of grassroots organizing. The leaders have been able to enhance and deepen the engagement of local citizens through connections with University of Minnesota Extension faculty who helped facilitate focus groups as part of "Community Speaks/MCHI Listens," an information-gathering project. In addition, the group's credibility and visibility have been helped by having its offices housed in a former church rectory that is in a residential neighborhood, across the street from a school, in the same building as a juvenile law enforcement base.

When You Go

Recruiting and organizing volunteers can be a big job. In some ways it's a lot like managing employees, only the compensation for volunteering is primarily intrinsic. Some initiatives thus find that they really need a dedicated volunteer coordinator.

Regardless of whether you have a coordinator, if you plan to actively recruit volunteers for your initiative see if you can find some help. Investigate whether your community has an active volunteer bureau that can help. Also consider making presentations to parent-teacher organizations, middle and high school service clubs, businesses, civic groups (such as Lions or Rotary), congregations, and youth-serving organizations. Senior citizen centers are another invaluable and often overlooked resource. When you are out talking with potential recruits, you can ask them to complete the "Time and Talents Discovery Form" on page 74 as a way of helping match their talents and interests with your initiative's needs.

Questions to Consider

There are a lot of ways that volunteers can work within an initiative. To start your planning, you may want to talk over some important questions:

► Which tasks on your action plans could be completed with the help of volunteers? Organizing events? Making phone calls? Assisting with mailings? Developing a Web site? Think easy, short-term for busy or apprehensive people, and long-term, in-depth for those who are more enthusiastic and have the time.

► How do you want to recruit? Do you need job descriptions? Do you want to advertise the positions, or call on people you already know? Will you require training or experience?

► Do you want or need a screening process? Will volunteers interact with young people and thus perhaps need background checks? Will you interview all volunteer candidates?

► How will you ensure diversity among your volunteers? Will you reach out to people who aren't typically thought of as volunteers (those with disabilities, English language learners, seniors, children, and so on)?

► How will you deal with barriers, such as transportation, language, and child care, that keep some people from getting involved?

► Once recruited, how will volunteers be informed of the tasks they are to do, the time involved, the location, the goals of various projects, and the training requirements?

► What will your evaluation process be?

► How will you let volunteers know that their contributions are valued?

Recruit and Organize Staff

Staffing is an issue every initiative must deal with. Few initiatives have more than two paid staff people—one appears to be the norm—and some have no paid staff at all. When the framework was first gaining momentum as a mobilizing tool, the staffs in many initiatives were people who took on the work as part of or in addition to their current positions. These included school prevention coordinators, youth workers, and human service professionals. Increasingly, community initiatives are creating paid coordinator positions.

As the Crow Flies

A key to successfully engaging volunteers is having a range of options available in terms of length, focus, and intensity of commitment. Some people might get really jazzed about helping plan a youth summit, while others might want or need to work from home making phone calls, stuffing envelopes for mailing, or other administrative tasks. When you think of asset-building actions think of the whole range of possibilities, not just direct contact with young people.

Time and Talents Discovery Form

Our community's asset-building initiative is seeking volunteers. If you would like to support our efforts to build Developmental Assets for and with children and youth, please fill out this form and return to
_____. Someone will contact you regarding your interest.

Name: _____

Address: _____

City, State, ZIP:_____

Phone:_____

E-mail: _____

Best time and day to reach you:_____

Best times and days for you to volunteer: _____

Why are you interested in volunteering for this initiative?

What skills and interests would you most like to use or develop through volunteering?

What talents would you bring to this initiative?

Is there a particular task or project that interests you? What is it?

What concerns do you have about volunteering?

What other comments or questions do you have?

Integrated Priorities, Funds Help Staff Initiative

The Stevens County, Minnesota, Healthy Communities • Healthy Youth initiative operates under the umbrella of the local mental health collaborative and the family services collaborative (both of which are funded in part by federal funds channeled through a state agency). The initiative coordinator reports to the director of community education. Thus, the Developmental Assets framework is being integrated into many different types of work with children, youth, and families. For example, as part of Early Childhood Family Education (ECFE), parents receive information about assets and participate in various activities that help them think about the practical implications for their families. There are also steps being taken toward having mental health included in preschool screening because, as past HC • HY initiative coordinator Char Zinda says, "Kids who have mental health problems early on are the ones who are most likely to have juvenile justice issues later." And Zinda, who is still an active initiative member and asset champion, says she's pushing for a mentoring program, including a paid coordinator, for young people just entering the juvenile justice system. "To me that seems [an] appropriate [use] for mental health dollars."

When You Go

Position descriptions are immensely helpful when it comes to staffing. Whether you have paid or volunteer workers, they'll be better able to do their jobs if they know what's expected. A position description is essential if you are hiring a paid coordinator, and desirable for all volunteers including coordinators, leadership group members, and task force participants. It can be a big task, though, developing and updating descriptions. You may want to have one person who is in charge of them. A creative solution might be to recruit a high school or college business class to draft them for you. They might welcome this kind of real-life project.

If your staff is entirely volunteer, make sure you build in strategies for maintaining momentum and consistency. If turnover is high, the initiative itself can become unstable. Similarly, it's important to tend to the spirits of paid staff to ensure that they remain positive and encouraged. The "work" of asset building is never finished. There is always more we can do individually and collectively. The result is that driven, focused people can run themselves ragged trying to accomplish as much as they can. In addition to enthusiastic supporters, they need professional development opportunities, recognition for what they accomplish, and peers with whom they can share ideas and solve problems.

Use or modify the "Staff/Volunteer Job Description Form" on page 76 to help you create position descriptions for any staff or volunteer with a formal role in your initiative.

Questions to Consider

➤ Is having paid staff a priority for your initiative?

➤ How could you fund a staff position(s)?

➤ Could members of your initiative do some of the work of the initiative as part of their current jobs? How would you make that happen?

➤ Is there a local funder who might be willing to provide support for a staff position? If so, how might you approach that funder?

As the Crow Flies

Staff transitions can lead to turbulent times for initiatives, especially those with only one or two paid employees. When an outgoing staff member has been well liked and successful there is often pressure on the incoming person to "live up to" the legacy. When a staff member leaves under uncomfortable circumstances the person coming in faces the challenge of helping others renew enthusiasm, put negative experiences behind them, and discover new ways of working together. In any case, taking the time and effort to acknowledge transitions and the inevitability of change will help ensure a good result in the long run.

Staff/Volunteer Job Description Form

Date: _____

Title: _____

Primary responsibilities: _____

_____

_____

_____

_____

Skills and experience required: _____

_____

_____

_____

_____

Skills and experience preferred: _____

_____

_____

_____

_____

Responsible to: _____

Hours per week/length of commitment: _____/_____

Reach Out

Embracing asset building in a community can pose an interesting dilemma. The ideas behind it (supporting and nurturing young people, building relationships, focusing on the positive) typically appeal to people who have already been doing many of the things that asset building is all about. But part of the power and beauty of the framework is that it provides a way to engage many people—indeed, *anyone* can build assets and *any* young person can experience assets. Therein lies the rub: how much time do asset champions spend trying to get the word out vs. sharing new ideas and inspirations with those who are already on board?

The answer, as usual, is that there needs to be a balance. But outreach is absolutely essential if your focus is truly on lasting, systemic change.

What's With the "Artitude"?

When a teacher at Mesa High School in Arizona noticed Alvino Martinez drawing his way through class (and not paying attention to the lesson), he referred him to the school's service-learning coordinator. The point was not to punish Martinez, but to capitalize on his passion for art by recruiting him to help spray-paint murals in the school bathrooms. In addition to getting to do something he loved (create works of art), the connection led to Martinez's eventual involvement with the Mesa Youth Leadership Alliance, a citywide youth development program.

When You Go

As with most aspects of asset building, the best way to *get started* is to build relationships. By listening to peoples' needs, interests, and concerns, and then sharing information about what you're doing, you build connections and trust.

This kind of outreach will, however, only go so far. For wider impact consider planning events or campaigns that will reach large numbers and wide varieties of people. Initiatives have used town meetings, celebrations, and presentations at existing events. New people are more likely to come if they are convinced they have a vested interest in what's happening (such as hearing the results of surveys of young people in the community).

Even if you use both of these strategies, however, you still won't reach the hardest-to-reach members of your community. For those who are least likely to join you on their own, consider recruiting asset champions who you believe can get to those who are most disconnected from community life. Charge them with making as many personal contacts as possible. For help in building outreach, see the worksheet "Developing an Outreach Plan" (on page 78).

Questions to Consider

➤ What outreach successes have you already had that are cause for celebration?

➤ Who are you most trying to reach? Why?

➤ Who are the people already connected with your initiative who could reach out to those who are not connected?

➤ Are there concerns, biases, or assumptions related to outreach that your leadership group needs to address? If so, what are they and how will you address them?

➤ Are there organizations within your community that already do significant outreach to hard-to-reach people? Could you learn from or get help from them?

For More Information

The Possible Dream: What Families in Distressed Communities Need to Help Youth Thrive (Search Institute, 2000).

As the Crow Flies

Reaching out doesn't necessarily mean making cold calls or knocking on doors. E-mail is one great way to initiate new relationships. A simple note telling a person what you're all about and that you'll be calling in a week with more information is fast, easy, and often effective as a first step. Volunteering in another organization is also a potentially "lucrative" strategy for meeting people who might be interesting in helping you build assets.

Developing an Outreach Plan

☐ Identify the purpose of your outreach (e.g., to build your initiative's core group, to build more assets for more young people).

☐ Decide which populations you want to target and why.

☐ Identify the environments in which you are most likely to connect with your target populations.

☐ Choose a number of outreach methods to try; experiment with them simultaneously.

☐ Evaluate which strategies are working and which are not. Keep those that work, drop the others, and add some new ones.

☐ If you are having trouble reaching one or more of your target populations, consider holding conversations with a number of leaders or representatives of those groups to get their feedback and suggestions on how to proceed.

☐ Continue on an ongoing basis to plan your strategies, implement them, evaluate them, and revise your plans.

Celebrate

Celebrations take many different forms ranging from sharing a cake at a meeting to holding a community-wide festival. Regardless of how you do it, it's important to take time to recog-nize and honor the achievements and progress of an initia-tive. It affirms the work that has been done, and can lead to renewed energy and enthusiasm.

Celebrating Teen Power

Celebrations offer hope, facilitate healing when needed, and give concrete ways to show that progress is being made. They can also be fun and add levity to a process that can at times feel over-whelming. Celebrations can be part of other events (such as meetings or community festivals), or they can be devoted to celebrating, as in Roswell, New Mexico, where the community held an event called "Teen Power! ¡El Poder de Juventud!" It included an exhibit of audio self-portraits installed in personal stereos, a "low-rider" bike show, youth art traveling on city buses, and murals decorating the local hospi-tal, a museum, and a printing company.

When You Go

Some celebrations are spontaneous and unexpected, but most will need to be intentionally planned. Even as you are developing your timeline you can be thinking about celebrations on two levels: within your initiative and in the community at large. It's sometimes easier to think of large-scale community events than it is to create authentic celebrations on the initiative level.

The key is authenticity. Be real! Do things that are fun, in the spirit of the person or event being recog-nized, and consistent with your overall vision, mis-sion, and goals. You may want to consider putting a person or committee in charge of celebrations and milestones. Some people really enjoy and have a flair for this kind of planning. Review the "Reasons to Celebrate" and "Questions to Consider" that follow to help jump-start your thinking. Then use the work-sheet "Celebration Planning" (on page 80) to help mark your milestones.

Marking Milestones

Milestones are significant events in the process of creating and sustaining an initiative and an asset-building community. While many mile-stone recognitions are celebratory, others are more subdued or even somber, such as when a major grant proposal is turned down. It's appro-priate, even important perhaps, to take time to-gether to acknowledge both the highs and lows of your collective action.

Reasons to Celebrate

- ➤ After naming your vision and mission
- ➤ When an action plan is approved
- ➤ When as asset builder takes action
- ➤ When an event goes well
- ➤ When a young person succeeds
- ➤ When an adult's attitudes about young people are transformed for the better
- ➤ On an anniversary or other important date for your initiative
- ➤ When a new partnership is formed
- ➤ When an evaluation is complete
- ➤ When a system is improved

As the Crow Flies

Some of the most fun, memorable celebra-tions involve relatively few people. Particu-larly when starting a new tradition, focus on the people who are there, not on how many aren't there. If your celebration is genuine and enjoyable others will hear about it and want to join you the next time around.

Celebration Planning

Reason for celebrating:

Task	Person(s) responsible	Issues to address	Completion deadline
Brainstorm ideas for type of celebration			
Determine budget			
Choose type of celebration			
Determine and secure location			
Plan menu			
Make food arrangements			
Develop list of invitees			
Prepare and deliver invitations			
Publicize event			
Recruit hosts			
Make sure all details are finalized			
Prepare and administer celebration evaluation			
Compile evaluation data			
Discuss planners' reactions to the celebration			
Make recommendations for future celebrations			

Questions to Consider

▶ Which milestones are important to recognize and celebrate in your process of creating an asset-building community?

▶ How can you celebrate the contributions of individuals without causing others to feel overlooked or underappreciated?

▶ What strategies can you use to increase the celebratory nature of things you already do (such as newsletters, team meetings, or special events)?

▶ How much time, energy, and other resources do you have to commit to celebrations?

Activate Sectors and Invigorate Programs

All organizations and sectors in a community—including schools, congregations, neighborhoods, youth-serving organizations, social service agencies, health-care providers, and employers—can be vital, active participants in your initiative. Organizations and leaders may need help, though, in discovering ways to activate their asset-building power and potential.

Wheel of Fortune

Before going after and winning a federal grant, the Northeast Community Challenge Coalition (NECC) in Ohio, was " . . . already working on assets but didn't have the funding to implement a community-wide initiative in a way that would be effective," says Coordinator Loretta Novince.

We knew we needed to go beyond simply building relationships and look at how each sector could foster the healthy development of children and teens by increasing protective factors against risky behaviors. The Developmental Asset framework provides opportunities for community sectors to go beyond relationship building to foster environments that send consistent messages about expectations for appropriate boundaries and provide opportunities for children and youth to develop the social competencies and values they need to grow up to be competent caring, responsible adults. The grant provided a wonderful opportunity to engage multiple sectors in using

multiple strategies to reduce risk factors and increase protective factors for children and youth, families, and the community.

Reflecting their vision of widespread engagement and impact, NECC's logo is a drawing of a wheel. The spokes identify the 12 target sectors ranging from youth to parents to law enforcement. The outer ring bears the equation "Education + Prevention + Healthy Lifestyles = Healthy Community." The federal grant proposal spells out how each sector will be trained in the asset framework in order to promote protection and reduce risk. "Because without a healthy community and healthy families," says Novince, "you cannot have healthy children and youth."

When You Go

Asset builders have found creative and inspiring ways to infuse asset building into sectors and organizations, and to bring these groups on board with community-wide initiatives. Here are some examples:

▶ Focus on the shared vision of a better, stronger, healthier, more asset-rich community.

▶ Network, network, network.

As the Crow Flies

In the national Healthy Communities • Healthy Youth initiative, congregations and schools have been the most significant "sector" players. Search Institute has developed entire lines of resources for both groups. We've found, though, that even within these groups it is sometimes difficult to facilitate co-operation between individual organizations. In the best situations, the enthusiasm grows out of the sector itself because of seeds planted along the way.

► Form a "barnacle coalition" by attaching asset building to great things that are already in motion within sectors and organizations.

► Show organizations and sectors how to enhance the asset-building potential of existing programs.

► Help organizations and sectors think about family-friendly policies and practices so that their employees, employees' families, and customers can engage in asset building in their own spheres of influence.

► Focus on one sector at a time rather than trying to draw everyone in at once.

► Identify sector and organizational champions (one or two asset champions working within specific sectors and organizations).

Questions to Consider

► What barriers will potentially interfere with engaging organizations and sectors?

► How can you deal with these barriers?

► What sectors and organizations are already well represented in your asset-building efforts? Schools? Government? Congregations? Health care? Law enforcement? Juvenile justice? Business? Military? Whom else do you hope to engage?

► What are the ways that sectors and organizations already connect in your community? How can you capitalize on those existing connections?

For More Information

Search Institute offers extensive resources and trainings for infusing asset building in schools, congregations, and youth-serving organizations. Here are a few:

Walking Your Talk: Building Assets in Organizations That Serve Youth (Search Institute, 2002).

Powerful Teaching: Developmental Assets in Curriculum and Instruction (Search Institute, 2003).

Building Assets, Strengthening Faith: An Intergenerational Survey for Congregations (www.search-institute.org/congregations).

Influence Civic Dialogue and Decisions

Asset-building change happens one person at a time. Reach enough people, however, and the community really does begin to feel transformed. Those who have caught the vision begin acting differently. Beyond their interactions with young people, they may alter many other things about their lives: where they walk, wheel, or run; where and how they shop; how they invest and/or make financial contributions; how they work; what they talk about with friends and neighbors; and, maybe, how they engage in civic life.

Making Change One Voter, One Funding Source, One Plan at a Time

Trainer and asset champion Keith Pattinson of British Columbia says that when he first began working with asset builders he found himself wanting to fix problems. With experience came a shift to wanting to change communities. Now, he says, he has "come down to wanting to change people."

In British Columbia there are 20 asset-building initiatives. In early 2004, representatives gathered in Vancouver to spend three days planning and strategizing. One organization taking the lead in that effort was the Royal Canadian Mounted Police (RCMP). The RCMP trains nearly all of its senior officers in asset building because one of its priorities is to increase their rapport with families and children. One result of the exposure to the framework is that some officers are now giving out "tickets" for positive behavior such as wearing safety helmets while biking. The officers, says Pattinson, are having more fun in their jobs because they are making positive connections with all young people, not just those in crisis or trouble.

South of the border, the San Luis Obispo Youth Task Force lobbied for government financial support of asset-building programs. In 1998, the group—including teenagers—approached its city council with the request. The city now sets aside $15,000 a year for asset-building grants of up to $5,000. The presence of the youth was significant, says network co-chair Richard Enfield, because "When teens that are really together go to a government body and do a good job of presenting their case, it's less of a hard sell than you might think."

And on the other side of the continent, in Hampton, Virginia, Mobilization for Youth has worked with city government to incorporate asset building into the city's strategic and neighborhood plans. It helps that some city officials there serve on the initiative's leadership team.

When You Go

There are many ways to influence civic decisions, but it's not always clear how to get started. To help, the Youth Advisory Council for the annual 2003 Healthy Communities • Healthy Youth conference created a CD of resources designed to provide communities, and young people in particular, with concrete steps they can take. Much of the material was excerpted or adapted from *Making Your Case,* written by the Minnesota Governor's Council on Developmental Disabilities (2001). For example, one concrete step is political campaign work. For a few more examples of concrete steps, see the handouts "Letters to Elected Officials" (page 84) and "Writing for the Editorial Page" (page 85).

Political party affiliation is particularly important to elected officials when: (1) organizing the government after an election—at which time the majority party takes control and members of the majority and minority have a voice in selecting their leaders and setting the direction and focus of their party (or caucus), and (2) when running for election or reelection. For the most part, the former is an internal process in which you will have little, if any, impact (nor should you). The latter, however, presents an opportunity for you to become fully involved.

If you have a strong political point of view, plan to work on the campaign of a candidate who will support and articulate that point of view. Surprisingly to some, campaign work—both for the candidate and for volunteers—involves a lot of grunt work. Stuffing envelopes, dropping literature, door knocking throughout the community, making telephone calls, and helping with fund-raisers are just a few of the tasks. However, the anticipated victory and camaraderie usually make it worthwhile.

And do not forget to make a financial contribution if you can afford it. Even a modest contribution

is always appreciated. During the campaign, you will have established a positive relationship with the candidate, and when he/she takes office, this relationship will allow you greater access. Politicians remember their supporters and workers.

Questions to Consider

► Which of your asset-building allies also have influence and visibility in your community? How can you capitalize on their power and connections?
► What type of influence do you want to have on civic decisions? Do you want to be an advocacy group? Or are your interests focused more on grassroots action?
► Do all of the people affiliated with your initiative exercise their right to vote? If not, why not? What can you do to get them to the polls?
► What are the hottest issues in your community that have an impact on children and youth? How can you engage members of your initiative in the discourse surrounding those topics?

For More Information

Making Your Case is available for download at www.mncdd.org/prof-adv/index.html.

As the Crow Flies
It seems the larger the community, the more layers there are in the civic decision-making process. People who grew up in large metropolitan areas might be surprised at how easy it is to connect with civic leaders in smaller suburbs and towns. Sometimes just a phone call to a mayor or city council person is all it takes to get on her or his calendar, even in a first-ring suburb. In bigger cities you may have more impact if you hook up with recognized neighborhood or issue leaders.

Letters to Elected Officials

Letter writing is probably the most widely used means of communicating with policy makers—who do pay attention to their mail. Elected officials readily acknowledge that a good letter—particularly from a constituent—can make an impact. That is why it is so important that your letter is powerful. The following guidelines will help to ensure that your letter will have maximum impact:

- The letter should be brief, preferably one or two pages (at the very most). Unfortunately, some people who feel strongly about an issue may have an irresistible urge to tell "the whole story" and believe the recipient must have all the details. Usually that translates into a long letter. Resist the urge. Keep your letter short.
- A form letter, preprinted card, or other superficial means of communication has little effect. If it's from a constituent, it may have some impact; others should forget it altogether. A well-written letter, however, can be e-mailed or sent through the postal service.
- If you are writing about a specific bill, include the bill number and a brief statement on the subject matter at the beginning of the letter. Because thousands of bills are introduced each session, it is impossible for individual leaders to track all of them. You can learn this and other specific information through the Internet.
- Discuss one bill or issue in your letter. This makes it far easier to track. If you wish to comment on several issues, write a separate letter for each.

- Your letter should be neat and your tone sincere and polite. Guard against being whiny or maudlin; do not threaten or belittle.

Your letter will have maximum impact if it contains the following components:

- A brief statement (10 words or less) on the subject; bill number if writing on a specific bill.
- An introduction of yourself that includes why you are interested in or concerned about an issue or bill.
- A personal anecdote about how the bill will affect you, your family, your community, your business, your job, your school, etc.
- Some facts, including supporting information and data to support your position.
- An invitation to contact you to discuss the bill, if desired.
- A request for a reply if you need one.
- A statement of appreciation for consideration of your position.

In addition to letters showing support (or opposition), elected officials receive letters requesting assistance to resolve issues with the bureaucracy. These requests usually are from constituents. In these letters, a leader is called upon to be an advocate or ombudsman. This role has expanded in recent years, and significant support staff exists solely to respond to these requests. If a politician is able to intervene successfully, the constituent is pleased. This is always important to any elected official.

Writing for the Editorial Page

Most newspapers and magazines have an opinion page that accepts letters to the editor or guest columns by community members expressing their ideas or beliefs on important social issues. This section of the paper is often called the *op-ed* or *opinion page.* Here are some tips to improve the possibility of your letter or article making the cut:

- Check with the editor of the opinion section to see if there are guidelines for op-ed pieces in terms of length, timing related to a relevant news event, deadlines, etc. (You may find this information printed at the end of the editorial section.)
- Make sure that your letter is neat and readable. If you have access to a computer or typewriter you may choose to type it. Double-spacing is the best idea for handwritten or typed letters. If your concern or idea is school- or initiative-related, use the appropriate stationery for an extra edge.
- Start your letter with: *To the Editor:*
- End it with: *Sincerely,*
  (Your signature)
  (Your name, typed or printed)
  (Your grade, school/organization)
- When writing the piece, define the issue or problem you are addressing in the first sentence. Note how the problem affects people—how many, where, who, and when. Your subject matter should be current.

- Clearly lay out your point of view on the issue and what you believe should be done about it. To keep your article organized and avoid rambling, identify no more than *three* key points you want to convey before you start writing. Never accuse anyone of anything without proof, or write anything that could get you in trouble.
- Remember that daily newspapers and consumer magazines are written for a broad audience with varying interests and education levels. Avoid using words that readers won't identify with or understand. Keep the language, supporting facts and figures, and argument simple and direct. Use your own personal experiences as a way to connect with your intended audience.
- Be sure to proofread and spell-check your final draft! Make your hard work as appealing as possible to the editor.

Plan and Facilitate Events

"Events" is an admittedly broad category. It can range from training, such as *Starting and Growing Your Asset Building Initiative* offered by Vision Training Associates, to celebrations like the Celebrate the Child festival in Ohio County, Kentucky, to annual road races like the one in Denver that raises money for and awareness of asset building. Despite the variation, there is some general information that can help you plan and organize successful events, regardless of the type.

Organized Chaos

"Give yourself more than two weeks to plan."
"Be sure to get the word out."
"Check your speaker's references."

While your travels may never take you to an international gathering in The Hague, chances are good that if you're involved in asset building you'll eventually engage in a summit of another sort. Youth summits are one popular type of asset-building events. Most are youth driven or entirely youth led.

Summits are a way to bring youth together to talk about issues, provide training and technical assistance, and develop concrete plans for change. For example, the Kettering (Ohio) Youth Council holds annual summits with young people fully engaged in the planning and facilitation. They describe these events as "organized chaos," and offer the tips listed above. Certainly there is a lot to think about and manage with this type of undertaking, but it's worth the effort, says Kettering's Alicia Budich. "Kids are amazing," she observes. "Given the opportunity to work with people, work with the community, it's amazing what we can come up with and accomplish."

When You Go

Enter into any event-planning process with caution. Events consume time and resources and thus the purpose and guidelines should be clearly identified from the start.

If you have determined that some sort of event is indeed a good idea, you can begin to think and talk about scope, dates, locations, agenda, publicity, and so on. Inviting others to help in this process can be advantageous. For example:

The media—Members of the local press may be able to help with planning. Or perhaps a recognizable media representative could be a speaker. At the very least they can get the word out and then attend the event.

Event planners—There are a lot of people who love planning get-togethers of all sizes. Some of them do it professionally. If you don't have someone with this expertise on your team, it's likely that someone involved has connections that can lead you to a person. Or you can contact local businesses and find out if they have anyone to recommend.

Designers and printers—They can help you develop invitations, programs, or handouts (or maybe they will print them for you at cost or for no charge).

Volunteers—You don't have to do it alone. Even people from outside your core group can be recruited to help manage the event itself. Consider having special name tags or T-shirts that make these resource people easily recognizable. And always remember to thank people who donate their time. Follow-up letters or cards ensure you don't miss anyone and can be good ways to reinforce the positive feelings they get from directly or indirectly building assets.

Once you have a team involved, here are some issues to consider:

What you want to accomplish—Your top priority should be to clarify your goals and intentions for the event. It's reasonable to simply want to give people an opportunity to come together and share ideas and information, but then the activities should reflect that. If you have a more specific set of objectives you'll want to be sure that your fellow planners agree.

Responsibilities—Everyone involved in leadership of the Kettering summits has a list of where he or she is supposed to be at what times. An event will take work and will be challenging. It will run much more smoothly if there is agreement about who is taking care of which details.

Location—Selecting a site depends on many factors: number of participants, technical needs, cost, and so on. The Kettering Youth Council recommends looking into low-cost locations that are unlikely to raise turf issues or to make students feel as if they are in school. Examples include community centers, conference centers, local colleges and universities, and senior citizen complexes.

Date and time—This will depend entirely on the time of year, the type of participants you want to attract, and competing events in the community. If you plan to include young people make sure you consult school officials to avoid conflicts with school-related activities. Also check with local leaders to find out when other community events are planned.

Food—Any time people (especially young people) are gathered for an extended period, it's a good idea to offer food, but the costs can add up quickly without some creative planning. Local bakeries, restaurants, or grocery stores may be willing to donate goods. And the food doesn't have to be outstanding. Also consider where and when it will be served.

To help you keep track of what you've done and what's left to take care of in planning an event, use the "Event Planning" worksheet (on page 88). Then to reflect on and document your experience, use the "Post-Event Summary and Evaluation" worksheet (on page 89).

Questions to Consider

▶ Why do you want to have an event? What are your goals?

▶ Who is your target audience for participation?

▶ What is the primary focus? Raising awareness? Motivation? Fun? Something else?

▶ Will you want media coverage? If so, how will you get it?

▶ Is an event the best way to accomplish these goals, reach this audience, and emphasize this focus area?

Create a Speakers Bureau

Many initiatives train cadres of people to deliver the asset message to the public. These are typically known as speakers bureaus. The idea is to have many people available to speak so any group interested in learning more about Developmental Assets can be linked with a knowledgeable, trained presenter. Ideally, links are made between groups and speakers who are familiar with one another or who share common characteristics (such as a teacher and a school group).

Multiple Benefits

The GivEm 40 Speakers Bureau of Traverse City, Michigan, has made nearly 250 presentations to community groups. The bureau, which includes adults and youth, strives to increase common understanding of the asset model and survey results. T. J. Berden, one of the founding youth members of GivEm 40, says being involved has impacted his speaking ability and comfort to the point that as a high school senior he presented to a crowd of 1,900 at the National Healthy Communities • Healthy Youth conference.

When You Go

Starting a speakers bureau can be quite simple. You need a group of people (including youth) who have some experience presenting to groups and who are willing to invest time in becoming articulate about the Developmental Assets framework. For the former, consider recruiting from your leadership group, other asset-building groups or organizations, student debate teams or clubs, speech classes, and Toastmasters. The best way to accomplish the latter may be to purchase *Speaking of Developmental Assets: Presentation Resources and Strategies.* It's a resource developed and published by Search Institute that includes

As the Crow Flies

One of the best ways to attract people to an event is word of mouth. It's simply more comfortable to attend something when you expect to see friendly faces. This will likely be more challenging for big-city initiatives than for those in smaller towns and suburbs. If you think that attracting participants will be a challenge, do what you can to make personal invitations: start a phone tree (like chain letters, only better); hand out fliers at other events and gatherings (rather than just posting them or having them available for people to take); and send e-mails to everyone on your list and sign the names of organizers.

Event Planning

Name of Event:

Date:

Description:

Person(s) primarily responsible for planning:

Purpose (goals):

How the event will achieve these goals:

How we will know if the event has been successful (objectives):

Desired number of participants:

Location:

Equipment/supplies needed:

Communication/publicity plan:

Post-Event Summary and Evaluation

Event name and date: _____

Location: _____

Members of planning group: _____

Number of expected participants: _____

Number of actual participants: _____

Factors affecting attendance (e.g., weather, lack of interest, conflicting events or schedules): _____

_____

Goal: _____

Describe each objective of the event, the results, and factors affecting the results:

Objective	Results	Factors affecting results

What worked best with the event?

What was the biggest disappointment?

Other comments:

Should a similar event be held in the future? Why or why not?

tips and scripts for presentations about the assets. If you have a small bureau you may be able to rotate one copy, or you may want to purchase several copies that can be checked out from one location.

You can also develop your own "standard" presentation and make it available to speakers, or invite them to prepare their own. In that case you'll be wise to screen for consistency and accuracy.

When speaking to groups within a particular context (schools, congregations, civic groups), tailored speeches are often more effective. For example, if you are speaking to a group of educators you can make sure you put particular emphasis on the asset-based research that ties to education and learning. You can pull stories and examples from your own schools, from this guide, or from other asset-building resources. If you are speaking to students you may want to focus a little less on the research and more on what they can do to make their communities better places in which to grow up. You can also include inspiring examples of young asset builders.

No matter what group of people you are speaking to, ask them if they are interested in youth and adult co-presenters. It's a great way to model intergenerational teamwork. And however you organize your bureau, it's best to have one key person to manage the resources, field calls, and schedule engagements. There are businesses that specialize in this area. Through the Internet or your yellow pages you may be able to find someone willing to help you with

planning, training, and logistics. If you have funding to pay them, they may be especially eager.

In *Speaking of Developmental Assets: Presentation Resources and Strategies,* authors Clay Roberts and Neal Starkman offer the following tips on making effective presentations:

► Try to arouse interest with the very first few sentences you speak. Offer an amusing anecdote, a startling fact, or a revelation about yourself.

► Help members of your audience focus by giving them an idea of what you'll be telling them.

► Mix up the media. Alternate visual aids with group discussion with an activity for pairs with reflection. The longer your presentation, the more leeway you'll have to make it interactive, but you can make a very interesting, interactive presentation in 25 minutes, too.

► Be as extemporaneous as possible. Consulting your notes is okay, but not at the expense of ignoring your audience. Remember, you can use transparencies or PowerPoint slides as your "notes"; they can help you find your way through your presentation.

► Engage audience members as much as possible. Tailor your examples to them, invite examples from them, ask them questions, and physically approach people. The more you can minimize the gulf between you and your listeners, the more likely your messages will be heard.

► Focus on people in the audience smiling or nodding at you; it will give you more confidence.

► Arrange participants into pairs whenever you want them to interact with one another. It's easy to get them into pairs. ("Everyone find a partner; try to find someone you don't know very well.") The activity goes quickly when only two people share, and people are more likely to be engaged and less likely to be threatened when they're asked to share with only one person. Encourage youth and adults to pair up whenever possible.

► Try to monitor three levels of your audience members:
    Thinking level—How much content are they taking in? Are you overwhelming them? Are you being too sketchy?
    Emotional level—Are they feeling something about the content? Are they excited?

As the Crow Flies

Eloquent, articulate teenagers are typically the most effective speakers when it comes to inspiring asset builders. Many teens, however, are just getting started on public speaking and can benefit from positive coaching and feedback. Before an actual presentation spend time planning and rehearsing. Invite a small group to sit in on a rehearsal so that it feels a bit like having an audience. And always after a presentation offer positive and constructive feedback.

Activity level—Have they been sitting too long? Do you need to provide an interactive activity?

▶ Adapt to unforeseen circumstances such as a controversial question or an antagonistic audience member. Acknowledge concerns, but try to bring the focus back to your messages. If you must, get the audience to work with you to quell a disruptive participant ("Does everyone agree that we've addressed this person's concerns as well as we can and that we should now move on?"), and always seek areas of agreement.

▶ Close with some intensity. Summarize what you've said, offer a challenge, and be inspiring. Leave your audience with something to remember.

Questions to Consider

▶ Why do you want to establish a speakers bureau?

▶ Who would be good spokespeople to involve? Will you involve people who have no previous speaking experience?

▶ What kind of information, training, support, and resources do you want to provide to speakers?

▶ Who will be responsible for coordinating the logistics of speaking engagements?

▶ Will speakers be compensated for their time?

For More Information

Speaking of Developmental Assets: Presentation Resources and Strategies (Search Institute, 2001).

 # Host a Link 'n' Learn

A Link 'n' Learn is a gathering of asset builders that focuses on informal networking opportunities. People who attend a Link 'n' Learn:

▶ Learn more about positive youth development, the asset framework, and the Healthy Communities • Healthy Youth movement;

▶ Learn new ideas about applying asset building;

▶ Energize their community's efforts to promote positive youth development;

▶ Reinforce their personal commitments to asset building; and

▶ Develop and strengthen their networks of support with surrounding communities.

North Dakotans Link 'n' Learn to Be Empowered

The Link 'n' Learn Youth Empowerment Summit in North Dakota brought together students (grades 8–11), teachers, counselors, and other adults from nine different schools. The daylong summit, facilitated by young people, focused on providing a forum for the following:

Connecting—Networking with youth in other schools and communities.

Changing—Understanding the concept of Developmental Assets as it contrasts with a problem-focused approach, applying the categories of Developmental Assets to their own experiences and perceptions, and making positive changes in their lives, schools, and communities.

Communicating—Empowering youth to carry the asset-building message back to their schools and communities by developing ads, songs, and posters.

Celebrating—Accepting the challenge of carrying asset-building messages to their schools and communities and celebrating asset-building strategies and actions that are working in other communities.

Participants learned about the Developmental Assets framework, HC • HY, the role of youth in local HC • HY initiatives, and spreading the word about Developmental Assets. They also shared ideas about how to get others involved in asset building.

 # When You Go

Search Institute has hosted Link 'n' Learn meetings since 1995. The term *Link 'n' Learn* reflects the spirit of connection and idea sharing that prevails at these events. There is no magic formula for success. Participation levels can be in the tens or hundreds; you can meet for a few hours or an entire day; and food can be available or you can brown bag it (or find a neighborhood cafe where you can share a meal and do more talking). Based on feedback from participants, we do know there are things that can help ensure the time spent together is productive:

► An effective Link 'n' Learn meeting provides a forum for those involved in initiatives to network and share learning. Participants are both learners and teachers. It's important to remember when planning a Link 'n' Learn that it is about information sharing. It is not a training event. Keeping this distinction clear for yourselves and for participants will help you get the most out of the experience. Participants should be encouraged in advance to share ideas, experiences, and stories.

► Participants will get the most out of the experience when their expectations align with their experience. Thus, it should be made clear that they will learn from the experience of others but will not receive consultation from an "expert" or a step-by-step guide to asset building.

► Time should be spent on introducing or reviewing the Developmental Assets framework. While many participants may know about and understand the framework, others will be new to it.

► If you want to involve youth in your meeting, you need to have youth on the planning committee. Their input will impact the whole agenda and flow of the day.

► If you will have a significant number of participants, you may want to plan for dividing the group into smaller, topic-specific "stations"

As the Crow Flies

The first Link 'n' Learns were relatively small, informal gatherings held in and around the Minneapolis area—Search Institute's home base. Smaller Link 'n' Learns can actually be an advantage in larger cities. Creating a close, neighborhood feel can give participants a sense that this is real, part of their lives and the community, and that it's happening right in their backyards. In contrast, in smaller towns, larger Link 'n' Learns that draw from other areas of the state can help people understand that this is bigger than just a nice but provincial idea.

around tables or in different rooms. Examples of topics that many asset builders are interested in are youth engagement, funding, raising awareness, and sustaining enthusiasm. Local experts and resource providers can be brought in to help with these conversations, but they should not monopolize the conversation. Another way to share knowledge and expertise is by providing display tables where people can showcase samples or presentations of their work.

Here's an overview of what to do and consider:

► *Identify your audience*—For some topics a wide audience is appropriate. Building positive youth-adult relationships, for example, will be of interest to any adult who works with or simply cares about young people. Many young people will also care about this issue. There are other topics, though, that will be of importance or interest to specific audiences. Initiative leaders and program planners may have a particular need for funding ideas; leadership teams may be interested in learning about different models of initiative management.

► *Clarify audience needs and interests*—Once you've identified your target group(s), you can talk with representatives to further pinpoint your topic(s). You can also check with them about times that work best. You may learn, as did members of the Minneapolis Uniting Congregations for Youth Development (UCYD) team, that Wednesday nights are bad for many youth workers affiliated with Christian congregations. Or perhaps you'll discover that there is an existing network that meets regularly on Friday mornings.

► *Plan the agenda*—Keep in mind when scheduling the day that conversations almost always take longer than expected. Avoid the temptation to pack the time too full. If you are inexperienced at planning events and would like some assistance, you can probably find people in your community who organize meetings or events and would be willing to help. Many businesses and organizations have people who specialize in this area. Those who work in public relations might also have experience planning and hosting events.

▶ *Publicize*—Invite too many participants. Realize that in most cases many people who know about the event will not come. Some will have conflicts, some won't be interested, others will be reluctant to join because they'll question whether they "belong" there. You can reduce the odds of these things happening if you get information out plenty far in advance, make it clear who the event is for, and make follow-up calls or other personal contact with as many invitees as possible. Sometimes a personal connection is enough to make the difference in whether someone chooses to attend.

To help you plan, prepare for, and host your own Link 'n' Learn, use the worksheets and handouts on pages 96–100. This information is also available online at http://www.search-institute.org/communities/downloads.

Questions to Consider

▶ What are your goals for your Link 'n' Learn?
▶ How will your planned activities help you accomplish those goals?
▶ Is there anyone in your area or with whom you have contact that has hosted a Link 'n' Learn in the past? If so, have you asked for advice or guidance?
▶ Are there others in the community who could help?

Train Asset Builders

Asset-building training is often really fun. Most trainers focus on the core ideas behind the framework: focusing on strengths, nurturing human development, and building relationships. The results are events that give participants the knowledge and skills to build assets and champion the asset-building movement. They also energize people, renew their commitments to young people, and offer networking and team building opportunities.

California Educators Trained for Asset-Building Action

Search Institute trainer Clay Roberts knows all about travel. During a call from his cell phone as he boards the car ferry that will take him to his Seattle home, he reports that he has been on the road all week, leading asset-based trainings for educators. He just has time for a quick interview before repacking his suitcase and heading off to the airport on his way to his next training destination.

Roberts has come from California where hundreds of educators are being trained in the Developmental Assets framework, and hundreds more are trained as trainers. From memory, he can recite the phone number of Linda Kearns, one of the forces behind California educators' growing awareness of and passion about asset-building schools. She's the coordinator of Drug/Violence/Tobacco/HIV Prevention Programs for the Orange County Department of Education. Since 1999, when Search Institute President Peter Benson was a keynote speaker at an annual conference on student health issues, Kearns has been coordinating a statewide effort to train educators in the asset model. Funding comes from the California Healthy Kids Program Office, a State Department of Education division focused on risk prevention and youth development.

Within 11 regions that include 58 counties, some of them divided by mountain ranges, Kearns has spread the trainings out across the state so as many people as possible can participate. The evaluations, she says, have been "phenomenal." So good, in fact, that many county offices of education have taken on asset building on their own, including scheduling additional trainings. This is significant, says Roberts, because these local offices "are where innovation and change happen. They provide a lot of resources to smaller regional districts who, because they cannot afford all the specialists they need, rely on county and regional service centers."

Potential Link 'n' Learn Sharing Session Topics

Surveys: Conducting the *Profiles of Student Life: Attitudes and Behaviors* Survey—Issues and Strategies

Building and Strengthening Local Asset-Building Initiatives

Mobilizing a Community for Asset Building: Leadership Structure, Planning, Communication, and Implementation Strategies

Getting Started: Mobilizing Sectors within a Community

Mobilizing a Specific Sector (e.g., education, congregations, youth-serving organizations)

Public Awareness: Community Strategies for Spreading the Word

Sharing Your Message with Diverse Audiences

Youth Involvement: Ways Youth Can Participate in Asset Building

Youth Involvement: Ways Youth Can Participate in Local Initiatives

Congregational Involvement in Your Community's Asset-Building Efforts

Intergenerational Approaches to Asset Building

Parent Education Ideas

Financing Your Initiative: Alternative Ways to Seek Funds for Your Initiative

Maintaining More Established Asset-Building Initiatives

Most Promising Practices (facilitated by local initiatives)

Momentum: Keeping It Going

Year Three and Beyond for Local Initiatives

Evaluating Your HC • HY Initiative

Creating Community Change: Models of Community and Social Change

Creating Community Change and Measuring Its Success

Neighborhood Strategies for Asset Building

Community Celebrations

Logistics of a Link 'n' Learn

You don't need a fancy or expensive facility to host a Link 'n' Learn meeting. Find a more economical facility to help keep expenses down, making the costs more reasonable and giving more participants the opportunity to participate.

Many planning committees have preferred settings such as schools, congregations, or community centers because these are often the places where the real work of asset building happens in their communities. These facilities also seem to feel welcoming and comfortable to many people.

Facilities that have worked well include: Community centers, K–12 schools, Colleges and universities, Congregations, Local businesses with meeting space, Libraries with meeting space, City halls or government centers, and Hospitals. Whichever type of facility you choose, it will need:

One main room large enough to hold all participants. Seating can be set up theater style (chairs, no tables), classroom style (tables with all chairs facing the front), or with round tables. Round tables with seating for eight or more are conducive to sharing among participants as well as with the larger group.

Three or four rooms large enough to hold 10 to 30 participants. These serve as breakout rooms for sharing sessions. Set up these rooms with chairs (with or without tables) in a circle. You may also use your main room as one of the breakout rooms, especially if you need to pay rent for each. Just ask participants to pull their chairs into circles.

A place to hold a meal. This may or may not be your main room. If you plan to provide food, make sure your facility will serve meals and refreshments for you, or that they will accommodate caterers.

Parking that is accessible and reasonably priced. Small inconveniences such as lack of parking or paying to park can really detract from participant enjoyment.

Other things to remember:
Arrange for audio and visual equipment as needed. Make sure tables are available for registration and any displays.

Make signs that indicate:
- Directions to get to rooms.
- Session names, to be placed on the room doors.
- Thanks to any sponsors of the event.

Link 'n' Learn Checklist

Event:_____

Date: _____

Location:_____

Planning contact: _____

Location contact:_____

Convene Planning Committee
☐ Call committee members.
☐ Determine location.
☐ Develop Planning Committee agenda and cover memo.
☐ Send Planning Committee agenda and cover memo.
☐ Prepare packets for Planning Committee meeting.
☐ Determine potential dates and locations.
☐ Determine presentation and sharing session topics.
☐ Identify potential facilitators and registration volunteers.

Secure Facility
☐ Reserve one room large enough for all participants.
☐ Reserve one breakout room per sharing session.
☐ Set up registration table.
☐ Set up tables for display materials.
☐ Make arrangements for refreshments from facility or caterer.
☐ Gather equipment.
☐ Determine costs.
☐ Get or prepare a map, address, and directions.
☐ Sign contract and send deposit, if applicable.

Publicize
☐ Design brochure.
☐ Print and fold brochures.
☐ Print labels.
☐ Get additional labels from local initiatives.
☐ Arrange for volunteers to label and tape brochures.
☐ Give press release template to local host initiative.

Coordinate Registration
☐ Write check number, amount, and date sent to accounting on registration form.
☐ Make copies of checks.
☐ Enter registrants into database.
☐ Develop a list of registered participants for a handout.

Determine Presenter and Facilitator needs
☐ Ask Planning Committee to invite potential facilitators to participate.
☐ Identify and invite presenters.
☐ Determine equipment needs.
☐ Confirm all volunteers, facilitators, and presenters.

Gather Materials and Supplies
☐ Participant roster
☐ Agendas
☐ Evaluation forms
☐ Folders for packets
☐ Search Institute products for packets
☐ Name tags
☐ Markers
☐ Pens
☐ Cash box
☐ Flip charts

Coordinate Follow-Up Activities
☐ Compile evaluations.
☐ Send compiled evaluations to Planning Committee.
☐ Send compiled notes to participants, along with thank-you cards.
☐ Staff review of compiled evaluations and best practices.
☐ Share best practices list with HC • HY listserv.

Registration

The invitation to a Link 'n' Learn meeting may be a letter, memo, or brochure that includes:

- Date, times, and location of the event

- What a Link 'n' Learn meeting is

- Who is invited

- Goals

- Agenda

- Registration fee

- Map to facility

- Acknowledgement of sponsors

- Registration deadline

- Payment requirements (e.g., "All participants must pre-pay to register.")

- Where and how to send the registration form and payment (your address and fax number)

- Request for information about which breakout sessions people want to attend (to help you predict room needs)

- Expectations of participants (e.g., "Please bring brochures or other materials your initiative has used to share with other participants.")

- A contact name and phone number (or e-mail address) where people can call to ask questions

Request Each Registrant's:

- Name, title, organization

- Address

- Phone

- Fax

- E-mail

- Age (youth or adult)

- Any special accommodations or dietary needs

- Permission to share contact information with other participants

- Method of payment

Suggestions for tracking registrations:

- Keep all copies of original registration forms.

- Enter the registration information into a database or spreadsheet.

- Create a registration form for the day of the event. Highlight people who owe registration fees.

- Bring a cash box to the event that contains enough change for anyone who is paying at the door, a receipt book with carbon copies, and receipts appropriate for collecting credit card payments (if you can accept credit card payment).

- If a participant needs to be invoiced for her or his registration after the event, make sure to get the billing address.

Link 'n' Learn Sample Flyer

Some meetings you attend . . . others let you connect.

LINK 'N' LEARN MEETINGS

Share, Learn, and Connect with Others Committed to Asset-Building in Your Area

---

WHAT is a Link 'n' Learn meeting?

The purpose of the Link 'n' Learn meeting is to provide a forum for learning and sharing among individuals or professionals involved in community mobilization efforts to support asset building.

At a Link 'n' Learn meeting you will:

- Get ideas from others involved in community mobilization in support of asset building for and with youth.
- Learn about strategies and actions that are working in other communities.
- Network with others facing similar opportunities and challenges.

- Be renewed to continue your work to promote asset building for and with youth in your community.

WHO should come to a Link 'n' Learn meeting?

The Link 'n' Learn meetings are designed for volunteers and staff who are organizing or leading efforts to mobilize their community or coalition of organizations in developing strategies and action steps to promote positive youth development.

Representatives from communities may come alone or as part of a delegation. Communities are encouraged to send teams of two or more representatives to this event.

We encourage youth participation in Link 'n' Learn meetings.
Let us know if young people are coming so that we can make a special effort
to involve them in ways that benefit everyone.

WHEN and WHERE
Ourtown High School
1234 Main Street
Ourtown, Ourstate 11111

CONNECT WITH LINK 'N' LEARN!

Follow-up Details after a Link 'n' Learn Meeting

General follow-up actions:

☐ Send out invoices that need to be paid.

☐ Pay all bills (e.g., facility, caterer, printer).

☐ Compile evaluation results to share with the Planning Committee.

☐ Type up notes taken during the meeting.

Ways to follow up with participants after the event:

☐ Make sure follow-up mailings include thanks to participants for their time, energy, and dedication to positive youth development.

☐ Send an updated participant roster.

☐ Send out meeting notes or minutes. Consider using e-mail or your organization's Web site to post these notes in a cost-effective way.

☐ If you have participants complete the "Most Promising Practices" summary, compile and mail the responses.

Ways to follow up with the Planning Committee members after the event:

☐ Send thank-you notes.

☐ Send a summary of evaluations.

☐ Send a questionnaire that asks about their satisfaction with the planning process and how it could be improved.

Most Promising Practices

Name of Link 'n' Learn meeting:_____

_____

Date: _____

Location:_____

What are three creative actions your local Healthy Communities • Healthy Youth initiative has done that have really proven to be effective? (*OR*) What are three things your community does well to help build assets in youth?

1.

2.

3.

If you could name one challenge your community faces when trying to build assets in youth, what would it be?

Name:_____

Community:_____

Please leave these in the center of the table. We will compile the lists and send them to participants three to four weeks after this Link 'n' Learn meeting.

When You Go

Search Institute, in partnership with Vision Training Associates, offers a variety of asset-building trainings. Some of these educational opportunities can be customized to be unique to a community, while others are "open enrollment," meaning they are held on a specific topic in a predetermined location and it is up to participants to arrange transportation and, if necessary, lodging.

The beauty of these trainings is that the impact reaches far beyond the participants. In Arkansas, for example, Initiative Coordinator Elizabeth Jones was working with an extremely tight budget but believed strongly that training was a priority. She decided to develop her own low-cost introductory training that would lay the groundwork for *Starting and Supporting Asset Building in Communities,* a Vision Training Associates session intended to deepen commitment to and understanding of asset building.

You may also find excellent training resources within your own community. You could consult with school administrators, representatives from local colleges and universities, youth development professionals, and others who may be able to offer specific recommendations.

Questions to Consider

- ➤ What are your training goals?
- ➤ Can these goals be best met by a one-time training event or an ongoing series?
- ➤ Whom do you want to train? Are they interested in being trained?
- ➤ What type of training has been offered in your community in the past? What was the impact?
- ➤ Who will take responsibility for planning and organizing training events? What resources does he/she need?

For More Information

Vision Training Associates:
http://www.search-institute.org/training/.

Use the Internet

In the early 1990s, when the asset-building movement was first beginning, Internet access was a growing trend but not yet particularly common. It seemed almost counterintuitive that a tool which allowed us to send and receive data without face-to-face contact could be an effective source of community building.

Today, however, the Internet is a major source of information, communication, and commerce. And as the use of the on-line chat rooms, discussion groups, Web sites, and other e-tools has grown, their role in asset building has also changed. There are now e-mail mentoring and pen pal relationships, extensive on-line catalogs of asset-building programs and resources, and other helpful and effective Internet uses.

A New Twist on Cyber Matchmaking

The Connecticut Assets Network (CAN) is focused so heavily on connecting asset builders across the country, and particularly within Connecticut, that coordinator Greg Ryan has dubbed himself a matchmaker. The initiative has developed a sophisticated, extensive Web site that allows users to search for initiatives, asset-building organizations, resources, and other information. Thanks to a fair amount of technical savvy, Ryan has managed to do this with the help of volunteers and a part-time paid assistant.

As the Crow Flies

We've heard many stories of "Aha!" moments—times when the Developmental Assets information first makes sense from a personal perspective—that occur during training sessions. Often it is when a trainer guides participants in reflecting on their own experiences growing up and the adults who influenced them. If you are designing an asset-building training or are hiring a consultant who is not steeped in the assets, make sure you emphasize the importance of "making it real" for people.

When You Go

It's likely that you'll have someone in your community, and maybe in your group, who has some experience planning and administering Internet use. This might be a great opportunity to pair a young person and an adult to work together. You'll want to first decide the scope of how you'll use the Internet: Do you want to assign someone to regularly search for information about asset building, youth development, and community development? Will you have an e-mail list, a discussion group, a listserv, a Web site? Would you like to be part of Search Institute's asset-building discussion group (www.search-institute.org/participate)? Do you want to be listed on Search Institute's Web site along with other asset-building communities across the nation (www.search-institute.org/communities/hchy.html)? Do you want to investigate ways to provide Internet access to those who don't have it at home? Be sure to connect your Internet plans back to your overall vision and goals. If you have a communication plan, it too should address the role of the Internet.

Once you've decided how and why you want to use the Internet, you can create an action plan. If you intend to develop a Web site, follow these tips:

▶ Build your site around your audience, not your initiative. Find out the needs and interests of constituents and potential audiences and keep that information at the forefront. It's likely that they'll get more out of the site if it focuses on what they can do and how they can get involved, and less on the structure and functioning of the initiative.

▶ Choose the content before you choose the format. While the format matters in terms of ease of use, the function should drive the form.

▶ Keep it simple. It's easy, particularly for people who are new to Web design, to make a site so complicated that it's not worth the time to try and navigate it.

▶ Link to other sites such as asset-building programs in your community, your local government, and Search Institute.

▶ If possible, update the site regularly. Identify which pages, such as the background information on assets and on your initiative structure, will remain the same, and which will be refreshed with new information, such as upcoming events, meeting announcements, and success stories.

▶ Don't worry about "doing it all." Your Web site is one tool for engaging people and keeping them updated on what's happening. It cannot effectively replace personal interaction and communication.

Questions to Consider

▶ Why do you want to use the Internet in your initiative?

▶ How can it help you accomplish your goals?

▶ Is there anyone in your group who has experience developing e-mail lists, listservs, or Web sites? If so, is that person willing to help you execute your plans?

▶ Will the Internet be an effective way of communicating with your leaders and constituents?

▶ Do the majority of people in your community have access to the Internet? If not, can you help them get it?

Form Task Forces

A task force is a group of people who work together for a specific purpose, often for a limited time. Engaging people in task forces gives them focus and goals to work toward, both of which can be very helpful in retaining or renewing enthusiasm. Asset-building task forces should, in all but the rarest of cases, be intergenerational.

So Little Time, So Many Models

While task forces typically report to an overseeing body, such as a leadership group, there are many different ways to structure and organize them. In Winter Park, Florida, for example, initiative member Luz Rivera led the establishment of what is called the Hispanic Task Force. The group focuses on engaging Spanish-speaking leaders and youth from the community to learn about assets, survey Hispanic youth, and develop strategies to mobilize the Hispanic community for asset building.

The LaCrosse, Wisconsin, initiative followed a very different track and formed one task force for each category of assets. A third model is used in Manchester, New Hampshire. There, four focused task forces (they called them "advance teams") emphasize four different key areas: schools, community, families, and communication.

When You Go

Here are four possible structures for organizing asset-building task forces:

Model A—Each task force focuses on strengthening each type of asset in the community.
Model B—Each task force focuses on a specific area, such as:
>   Communication
>   Evaluation
>   Celebrations
>   Training
>   Fund-Raising/Finance
>   Cross-Sector Partnerships
Model C—Each task force focuses on mobilizing and equipping a particular sector, such as:
>   Youth
>   Adults
>   Business
>   Neighborhoods
>   Congregations
>   Media
>   Family
>   Schools
>   Community Agencies
>   Health Care
Model D—Task forces are formed only to deal with specific needs or issues as they arise.

You may find that a different way of organizing works best for your community. If you decide that task forces, however organized, are a good idea for you, run your proposed structure past key stakeholders. Their impressions and reactions can help you move forward or make important adjustments. Once you decide to form one or more task forces, leadership and membership are your next issues to resolve. In some cases it will be obvious; a person or group of people will have a particular passion for or interest in an issue and they will become your group. Whether this is your situation or you have to actively recruit, develop short position descriptions

that include expectations, time commitments, and so on.

If you need or want help in determining whether and how to form task forces, consult with a person who has experience in organizational development. You can find these people in many environments, including human resource departments, businesses, and on boards of directors of nonprofit organizations.

Questions to Consider

> ➤ What needs do you have that might be best met by task forces?
> ➤ Would creating task forces help you accomplish your initiative goals? Why or why not?
> ➤ How many task forces do you need? How many people on each?
> ➤ Should your task forces be ongoing? Time limited? Or should duration depend on the issue?
> ➤ How often will task forces meet? Will that be in lieu of current initiative meetings?
> ➤ Can you ask people to make an additional time and energy commitment and still keep them enthused?

As the Crow Flies

Search Institute has had the unfortunate experience of referring constituents to a Web site that was once a reputable resource on adolescence but had been purchased by a company peddling teenage pornography. It was humbling and embarrassing, to say the least. Beware that people with harmful intentions sometimes use harmless sounding child- and teen-focused site names. Any time you link to or reference a site, check and double-check. And then consider adding a disclaimer like the one that appears in the beginning of this book.

Form Partnerships

One way to reach more people—and get more done—is to form partnerships with other groups or organizations. Partnering is different from networking in that the emphasis is more on what you can get done together, and less on the relationship itself. As always, though, the relationships are important and require attention.

Starting with a Solid Foundation

Effective partnerships are built on trust and respect between individuals. Success is more likely if all stakeholders participate in decision making and planning, and if the focus is on the pieces of the overall vision that the groups involved share. It often works well, once the basic connections are made, to start with something small like co-hosting a celebration such as the annual We Care about Kids Day in New Hope, Minnesota. The local YMCA provides the facilities, and two other groups—the area's asset-building initiative (Community Ahead) and the Mosaic Youth Center—help plan, organize, manage, and publicize the event. In addition, other youth- and family-serving groups in the community are invited to have displays or activities letting people know about their services and activities.

As the Crow Flies

Know when to hold 'em; know when to fold 'em. In other words, be clear with task forces about what's expected and when their commitment will end. People will be much more likely to stick with something (and perhaps to volunteer again in the future) if the boundaries established initially are honored.

When You Go

Through extensive research and experience, the Amherst H. Wilder Foundation has identified factors that contribute to effective collaboration between partners. Use the modified checklist "Forming a Successful Partnership" (on page 105) to assess what needs to be done to ensure success in your own partnerships.

Questions to Consider

▶ What do you hope your initiative and your community will gain through partnerships?

▶ With whom do you already have partnerships? What other relationships are fledgling and could be nurtured into partnerships?

▶ Are there fears or concerns about partnering that need to be addressed? If so, what are they and how will you address them?

▶ Who are the young people in your initiative or your community who can help make partnerships "come to life"?

For More Information

Building and Sustaining Positive Change (CD-Rom for Windows, available from Search Institute).

Pass Resolutions

Some initiatives find that drafting a resolution adds credibility to their efforts. City councils, schools boards, organizational boards, and other governing bodies can pass formal resolutions to officially endorse an action or a group. They are not generally effective as awareness-raising tools, but they do often pave the way for increased buy-in for your efforts, especially if they are not overused.

When You Go

Getting support for a resolution will probably take some networking on the part of key stakeholders within your initiative. By developing connections and relationships with school board members, city council representatives, and other members of

Forming a Successful Partnership

Environment

Is there a history of collaboration and cooperation between the potential partners?

☐ Yes   ☐ No

Is the political and social climate favorable to forming a partnership?

☐ Yes   ☐ No

Membership Characteristics

Do potential partners share mutual respect, understanding, and trust?

☐ Yes   ☐ No

Does the proposed partnership include an appropriate cross-section of representatives?

☐ Yes   ☐ No

Do people and organizations see the partnership as being in their self-interest?

☐ Yes   ☐ No

Do potential partners have a willingness and ability to compromise?

☐ Yes   ☐ No

Process/Structure

Do potential partners share a stake in both process and outcome?

☐ Yes   ☐ No

Are clear decision-making processes in place?

☐ Yes   ☐ No

Are the partnership processes and structure flexible and adaptable to changing needs?

☐ Yes   ☐ No

Are clear roles and policy guidelines in place?

☐ Yes   ☐ No

Communication

Is there open and frequent communication among partners?

☐ Yes   ☐ No

Have you established formal and informal communication links?

☐ Yes   ☐ No

Purpose

Does the partnership have concrete, attainable goals and objectives?

☐ Yes   ☐ No

Do the partners share a vision for the partnership? Is the purpose of the partnership unique in the community?

☐ Yes   ☐ No

Resources

Are there sufficient funds and other resources available to sustain the partnership?

☐ Yes   ☐ No

Does the partnership have a skilled convener?

☐ Yes   ☐ No

Follow-up discussion topics:
- What are the strengths of this potential collaboration?
- What areas need to be developed?
- How can we build on the strengths to deal with the areas that need developing?
- What should be our next steps?

St. Louis Park's Resolve

This is a resolution that was passed in St. Louis Park, Minnesota:

WHEREAS children and teenagers deserve to grow up safe, healthy, loved, secure, and well-educated, and

WHEREAS many families need support to meet the needs of their children in this stressful society, and

WHEREAS the St. Louis Park community is preparing to undertake a major effort called Children First to strengthen families and become a caring community for children, and

WHEREAS Children First focuses less on responding to crises and more on developing a community-wide infrastructure to surround children and adolescents with the wide range of assets that are crucial for healthy development, and

WHEREAS we recognize the interdependence of government, schools, businesses, social service agencies, civic organizations, and neighborhoods and thus believe the best way to ensure our children's future is to work together, and

WHEREAS because of its traditions, community spirit, and strong institutions St. Louis Park is uniquely placed to make these efforts succeed and to become a model for other communities throughout the nation,

NOW THEREFORE BE IT RESOLVED that the Board of Education of St. Louis Park endorses the Children First initiative by the St. Louis Park City Council, Independent School District 283, the Rotary Club of St. Louis Park and all of its citizens and businesses, and

BE IT FURTHER RESOLVED that the Board of Education invites and encourages school staff, parents, and all residents of St. Louis Park to join in this partnership benefiting children, teenagers, families, and ultimately each one of us.

Enacted on the 29th day of November 1993 and entered into the minutes of the proceedings.

Betty Shaw, Chair, Board of Education, St. Louis Park, Minnesota.

government, they can learn how resolutions typically come to be. This is an especially good time to call young people to action. If students approach the school board, for example, the members will likely be more intrigued than if a group of parents raises the issue. It's also potentially more newsworthy if young people are taking the lead.

Before approaching any governing body about the possibility of a resolution, clarify your focus and your purpose: Do you want to gain credibility for your initiative? How will a resolution help that? Are you are asking for an endorsement of your initiative, or of a focus on asset building in your community? Having your priorities clearly identified will help you make the case that the resolution is a good idea.

Questions to Consider

▶ Which governing bodies in your community could give your effort credibility by passing a supportive resolution?

▶ How will a passed resolution help you build assets for and with young people?

▶ Who can help you create a resolution?

▶ Which key people need to be contacted in the process?

Hold Town Meetings

Town meetings are a popular way to bring the Developmental Asset framework to the public and to generate interest in and support for an asset-building initiative. All citizens are invited to attend a public meeting where information is shared and questions raised and often answered.

Going the Extra Miles

Early in their community's asset-building efforts, leaders in Mankato, Minnesota, scheduled a town meeting. To increase accessibility, planning committee members arranged for sign-language interpreters, free childcare, and free bus service to the gathering. They ended up with 2,300 participants.

When You Go

It works well to schedule town meetings far in advance. This allows many people—politicians, business leaders, and citizens—to get it on their schedules before other things come up.

Once it's scheduled, many people will hear about the meeting through word of mouth. You can capitalize on this informal advertising by supplying a steady stream of newsletter articles, mailings, and notices in public places. You can also post information on your community's Web site and encourage local media to remind viewers, listeners, and readers. Your job communicating will be easier if you have a one-sentence purpose statement and two or three outcomes that you can easily articulate.

Planning the meeting itself can be an unwieldy job for someone not experienced in event planning. You may want to connect with your Chamber of Commerce, local government, or people who specialize in event planning. They can help you think about facilities, supplies, refreshments, and other details. For a sample agenda see the handout "Town Meeting Sample Agenda" (on page 108). For help in gathering information after the meeting, see the worksheet "Town Meeting Follow-Up Information" (on page 110).

Questions to Consider

► At which point in your asset-building efforts would a town meeting be most beneficial? As a kick-off event? To release survey results? To renew enthusiasm?

► Who will be most likely to come? Least likely?

► What barriers can you address to make it easier for people to come?

► Will you have speakers? Small group conversations? Question and answer sessions?

► Who would be good speakers or facilitators for the event?

Release Survey Results

The survey results we are referring to are those that measure young people's Developmental Assets or community attitudes regarding children and youth. The information here may also be helpful if you have data from other community surveys and are wondering how to handle their release.

There really is no one appropriate category under which to address this topic. Some community initiatives are launched after a school district administers a survey and releases the results. Other times people get very excited about the framework of assets and a survey isn't conducted until the initiative is already well established. Whenever and however the results are released, it can be a time for raising awareness about young people's needs and experiences, focusing on community priorities, bringing the community together, and encouraging people to build assets for and with young people.

As the Crow Flies

By now it's old news that young people often get relegated to token roles in partnerships. What's less talked about is that sometimes that happens because partnership development often takes a long time, and most young people move on after high school or even before their senior years. With lots of transitions it's difficult to keep things moving. A solution is to push forward without really taking the time to bring new people up to speed on what's happened and is currently happening. When thinking about young people to involve, consider "grooming" 8th, 9th, and 10th graders who may not yet be recognized leaders, but could have a lot to offer.

Town Meeting Sample Agenda

As people arrive, give them each a printed agenda, two 3 x 5 inch cards, and a blank sheet of paper.

Welcome
Ask a member of your vision team or other initiative or community leader to greet participants.

Introduction
Explain the purpose of the meeting (talking about creating an asset-rich community) and briefly review the agenda, letting people know what kind of participation will be expected of them. Then encourage participants to write questions they have on the note cards and turn them in at a designated spot (someone will need to collect these).

Strengths and Concerns
Ask participants to shift into small groups of three or four. Request that each group designate a recorder to take notes. Then ask them to discuss the strengths they see in the community when it comes to raising children and youth. After a while (depending on how much time you have) ask them to identify concerns they have about what it's like to grow up in your community. Finally, collect their notes about their conversations.

The Vision
Invite a member of your initiative to present your vision for the community.

Questions and Answers
With a number of leaders on stage or in front to answer questions, use the collected cards to start a group conversation. After key questions have been addressed, have an open microphone time when people can come forward to comment or request further explanation. Request that they observe two courtesies: speak one at a time, and for two minutes or less.

Next Steps
Provide information about the concrete, easy steps that people can take to start making a difference for young people. You can use the "Town Meeting Follow-Up Information" worksheet (on page 110) to collect information about potential supporters of and volunteers for your initiative.

Closing
Thank everyone for coming and encourage them to follow through on ideas they've had or commitments they've made. Assure them that each person in the community can make a difference.

Putting Youth "Out in Front" in Vermont

The Vermont Rural Partnership is a coalition of 18 schools in rural Vermont. All sites have measured students' Developmental Assets. Students have taken the lead in synthesizing and reporting on the data with the help of a *Guide for Student Analysis of the Search Institute Data: Organization of a Day Retreat for 6th through 12th Graders,* developed by Helen Beatty. In the introduction Beatty writes:

> Students are too often the recipients of well-intended, adult-driven decisions about their health and well-being. The implicit message is that they are not capable of being leaders and participants in positively shaping the world in which they live . . . When young people become the messengers for the data and how it can influence a future direction for the community at large, adults are presented with a compelling opportunity to value youth for their honesty, commitment, wisdom, visions, and capacity to shape a better future for us all.

Before the survey results are even in, it's important to determine who will present the findings and who should hear the data first. As Beatty notes, this is an important strategic point for including young people. Not only will the information be more compelling when coming from young people themselves, teens need a chance to react to and share their feelings and opinions about the findings.

Once the results are available, someone—preferably an intergenerational task force—needs to examine and discuss the data, identifying highlights. When these key points are identified, it helps to make them visual, using charts or graphs. While there are people who like and learn well from numbers, others need to see a "picture." Some of this will be included in the report you receive from Search Institute. Some you may want to develop to meet your own needs. It's fairly easy to create a one- or two-page handout with key information.

Often the data is initially presented to the people who were surveyed (usually students). For a sample, see the handout "Sample Summary of Survey Findings" (on page 112). Then, if it was conducted through the schools, a letter may be sent to parents. For a sample, see the handout "Sample Letter to Par-ents about Survey Findings" (on page 113). Many schools hold parent meetings to discuss the findings.

After young people, parents, and schools have had a chance to hear about and reflect on the survey results, a community may plan some sort of wider release of the information, such as a town meeting, public forum, news releases, or presentations to groups within the community.

Here are suggestions for presenting to specific audiences:

Students—Hold a school assembly, give a special presentation to the student government, and provide teachers with related information they can use in their classrooms. Also make the information available to the school newspaper or television or radio station.

School administrators—Hold smaller, personal discussions, expert roundtables, meetings with the superintendent, or presentations to the school board.

School faculty and staff—Present information as part of in-service teacher trainings or staff meetings.

Parents—Hold a special meeting, ask to be part of a regularly held meeting, or include the information in a newsletter or special mailing.

Community leaders—Make personal visits, send letters, and invite them to other events featuring the data.

Media—Send press releases and consider holding a press conference.

Anyone—Tie the data into small, simple things people can do to make your community a better place for young people to live and grow.

As the Crow Flies

Governments in small towns and suburbs are generally a lot more accessible than those in big cities. If you would like to pass a resolution but are having a tough time getting the support you need, consider changing your focus to a group such as a school board, community council, or other smaller governing body.

Town Meeting Follow-Up Information

☐ Yes! Tell me more about how I can make a difference for children and youth in our community!

☐ Add me to your mailing list to receive information about the asset-building initiative in our community.

☐ I would like to get involved in a task force that's working on building assets in our community.

☐ I have an idea for how to build assets in our community: _____

_____

_____

_____

_____

☐ I belong to a group that may be interested in learning more about the initiative: _____

_____

☐ I am particularly interested in: _____

_____

_____

_____

_____

Name: _____

Address:_____

City/State/ZIP: _____

Phone number: _____

E-mail: _____

Best day and time to reach me: _____

As you examine survey findings about your community, use the following questions to help you identify highlights and key points.

▶ What findings surprise you?
▶ What findings are most pleasing to you?
▶ What findings are most troubling?
▶ What differences do you see when comparing data by demographics (such as by age or gender)?
▶ From your perspective, what are the three most important findings?

Questions to Consider

▶ Who are the first people who need to hear and see the data? How will you engage them in presenting to others?
▶ What role will young people play in synthesizing and presenting the data?
▶ What methods will you use to present the data?
▶ How deep into the community will your communication efforts reach?

For More Information

What's Up with Our Kids? (Customized presentation offered by Search Institute).

Get the Word Out: Communication Tools and Ideas for Asset Builders Everywhere (Search Institute, 2002).

The Asset Activist's Toolkit: Handouts and Practical Resources for Putting Assets into Action (Search Institute, 2005).

As the Crow Flies

Truth be told, town meetings *can* be pretty boring. Particularly in larger communities, there's little motivation to get involved unless there is a specific issue (usually one of concern) that citizens want to see addressed. Since you've done some background work on your community's strengths, resources, and priorities, focus on topics that you know will generate interest. Asset building may not be at the top of the list, but once people are there they will hear about the power of assets to address many of the community's concerns.

Sample Summary of Survey Findings

Study Highlights from *Profiles of Student Life: Attitudes and Behaviors*
Ourtown, U.S.A.

In the fall of this year, 900 students in 6th to 12th grade in the Ourtown Public Schools were surveyed using Search Institute's *Profiles of Student Life: Attitudes and Behaviors* survey. A report on this study from Search Institute, a nonprofit research and education organization in Minneapolis, gives our community important information about our young people.

Experiences of Developmental Assets

Developmental Assets are external and internal factors that contribute to healthy development in young people. Search Institute has identified 40 of these assets.

- The assets our young people are most likely to experience include a positive view of their personal future (70%), family support (64%), involvement in religious community (64%), and school engagement (64%).
- The assets our young people are least likely to experience are creative activities (19%), community values youth (20%), a caring school climate (24%), youth as resources (24%), and reading for pleasure (24%).

The Power of Assets

These 40 Developmental Assets are powerful influences in young people's lives, shaping their behavior and choices. The surveys show that youth in Ourtown who experience more of these assets are:

- Less likely to engage in harmful or unhealthy behaviors; less likely to use alcohol, tobacco, or other drugs; less likely to be sexually active; and less likely to engage in violent or antisocial behavior. For example 61 percent of youth who have 0 to 10 of the 40 assets report being involved in violent behavior. In contrast, only 6 percent of those with 31 to 40 assets report engaging in violence.

- More likely to have positive attitudes and make healthy choices. In addition, young people with more assets are more likely to be successful in school, value diversity, maintain good health, and delay gratification. For example, only 7 percent of youth with 0 to 10 assets get mostly As in school, compared with 53 percent of those with 31 to 40 assets.

The Challenge Facing Ourtown

While these assets are powerful in young people's lives, too few young people in Ourtown—and other communities across North America—experience enough of these assets.

- On average, young people in Ourtown experience 18 of the 40 assets.
- The average girl in Ourtown experiences more assets than the average boy (18 vs. 16).
- Overall, only 20 percent of Ourtown's youth experience 10 or fewer of the assets. Another 42 percent experience 11 to 20. Only 38 percent experience more than half of the 40 assets.

Our Response

Most assets are nurtured by strong relationships between adults and young people and young people and their peers. Ourtown is committed to strengthening the asset base for all our children and youth. It will take everyone—parents, other adults, community leaders, young people—and every institution working together. What can you do to strengthen this critical foundation for our community?

Sample Letter to Parents about Survey Findings

Ourtown School District
222 Main Street
Ourtown, Ourstate 11111

[Date]

Dear Parent:

As you know, students in the Ourtown Public Schools recently participated in an in-depth survey called *Profiles of Student Life: Attitudes and Behaviors.* The survey measures, among other things, 40 Developmental Assets. These assets form a critical foundation for young people's growth and well-being. We have received a report on the findings, and I want to share with you what we have learned about our students.

Enclosed is a one-page overview that the Survey Task Force has prepared. Some things that I want to be sure you notice include:

- A strength is that most young people feel cared for and supported at home. We thank you as parents for this important contribution you make to our community.
- A concern is that too few of our young people experience enough of the Developmental Assets. Because the assets are so powerful in their lives, our youth need us to redouble our efforts to ensure they have the relationships, opportunities, strengths, and environments they need to succeed in life.

We know that parents cannot do this work alone. That is why Ourtown is working to unite the entire community around a vision of helping nurture these strengths in and for our young people.

I hope you will take the time to talk with your child about these findings. You can use the assets as a way to start an important, ongoing conversation about how your family helps your child grow up caring, responsible, and healthy.

Then, join me at 7:30 p.m. on October 14 in the high school auditorium to talk more about what these survey results mean for our community. This meeting will be an opportunity for community members to learn about the findings. Students, faculty, and experts will be on hand to present information and answer questions. We'll also talk about what we want and need to do in Ourtown to focus attention on building these assets for all of our children and youth.

I hope you will attend this extremely important gathering to learn firsthand what the data mean to our young people and our community, as well as to share your thoughts and concerns.

Sincerely,

Jane Doe
Superintendent, Ourtown Public Schools

Chapter 3

Culture and Customs

This section highlights what asset champions can do to create a community climate that nurtures and supports all children and youth.

Don't Miss It
► Enjoy the Ride
► Build Trust along the Way
► Deal with Issues of Safety and Liability
► Work Through Roadblocks

Optional Side Trips
► Get Media Attention and Coverage
► Go Further and Longer Than You Ever Thought You Could

Enjoy the Ride

Many asset champions have discovered that while the science of the asset framework is important, it's the joy and pleasure they get from the work that helps grow their enthusiasm. There's no question that building and sustaining an asset-building initiative is challenging but it certainly doesn't have to be difficult, frustrating, or boring.

Something Is Certainly Different Here

One autumn, the school staff at the senior high in New Richmond, Wisconsin, decided they wanted to kick off the year with something special and unique—a reflection of how they saw the school community. They also wanted new students to quickly realize that "something is different here," says asset champion and former New Richmond guidance Counselor Marilyn Peplau.

Each department was charged with coming up with a theme song that reflected their work, and then planning a lip-sync performance to go with it. One result was that as the students were sitting waiting for the first-day assembly to begin, the new principal and assistant principal rolled across the stage on a rumbling Harley. They were dressed from head to toe in leather and blasting through the auditorium was the song "Leader of the Pack." In addition to the administrators' dramatic entrance, the students were treated to the guidance office staff's version of "Lean on Me" and other "hits."

When You Go

To tell you how to have fun would be a bit like telling you what food you will like. Everyone has unique preferences, tastes, and perspectives. We know of a road race that focuses on assets, a play about "Asset Girl" that's used to teach people about the concept of an asset-building community, a youth summit structured around the theme of the *Survivor* television shows, and hundreds of community celebrations that focus on children and youth.

Fun need not be limited to special events or activities. Levity can be added to a team meeting by sharing fortune cookies with silly messages, playing music during a brainstorming session, incorporating coloring or other art activities into a task, or cheering for a recent accomplishment. Think big, small, and everywhere in between. Here are some suggestions for how to get the ideas rolling:

► Let young people take the lead.
► Make use of the resources (natural, cultural, social) available in and unique to your community.
► Incorporate movement or physical activity.
► Look for ways to engage all five senses. It will help people connect with asset building in their hearts and souls, as well as their minds.
► Keep humor respectful.
► Inform the media. If you're planning an event that is intended to be fun, it may be a good time to reach out to television and print media. Pictures and stories of entertaining celebrations or gatherings tend to draw more attention than meetings and other less exciting happenings.
► Make learning and teaching fun. Chances are that you'll develop some sort of cadre of speakers. Why not get them together and share ideas for how to increase the fun factor in their presentations?

Questions to Consider

► What are you already doing that's fun?
► How can you bring levity to your meetings?
► Are there entertainment events in the community with which you could collaborate or that could link to your initiative?
► What do young people in your community do for fun?
► What do adults in your community do for fun?

For More Information

Building Assets Together: 135 Group Activities for Helping Youth Succeed (Search Institute, 1997).
More Building Assets Together: 130 Group Activities for Helping Youth Succeed (Search Institute, 2002).
Creating Intergenerational Community: 75 Ideas for Building Relationships Between Youth and Adults (Search Institute, 1996).

Build Trust along the Way

Building trust among the key players is critical to building ownership and buy-in. When there is a high level of trust, teams, task forces, and asset-building experiences are more effective and more rewarding.

Lots of Ways to Build Trust

The GivEm 40 coalition brought together about 50 business leaders and 100 youth to have an open and honest conversation about the dynamics between the two groups. They ended up with a list of asset-based things they'd like to accomplish together.

The Red Lodge Youth Council in Montana takes advantage of its proximity to the Bear Tooth Mountains by taking youth and adults on guide-led backpacking trips. John Poore, the adult coordinator for the council, says that in addition to the natural educational opportunities that arise in this environment, the group makes a point of nurturing and exploring the interdependence that comes with youth-adult partnerships. For example, he says ". . . when an adult doesn't know how to start the stove, a kid who has gone [on the trip] two years can do it."

All trainers affiliated with the Alaska Initiative for Community Engagement help build buy-in and trust by following a simple rule: they never tell audiences what assets are. Instead they ask them what kids need. This, says former Coordinator Derek Peterson, always elicits assets out of the group so they own the wisdom instead of it being outside information.

When You Go

Trust is not something that happens overnight. It accumulates over time when individuals have positive experiences with one another. This can be difficult regardless of the makeup of the group. A highly homogeneous group may have an easier time since they share a lot in common; on the other hand, they may fear that others are trying to tread on their territory. Similarly, very diverse groups can find that their differences are stimulating and exciting, making trust building easier. Or they may discover that miscommunication and misinterpretation of actions and words are prevalent. The lesson in all of this is to not take trust for granted. An investment in trust building is well worth the time.

So what does it take? As usual, when it comes to change, there's no magic strategy. Trust building has a lot to do with decision making. Thus, you'll want to have a clear process from the start of your work. That will likely evolve as more people get involved and you build a shared history. But it's important nonetheless to be attentive to it early on.

Another way to build trust is to spend time getting to know one another. This can come from creating an environment that allows for open and honest dialogue, participating in team-building exercises, doing service together, planning social activities, and dedicating time at each meeting to icebreakers or other interactive activities. Youth workers, religious leaders, counselors, and others who work with people can be good resources for ideas about trust building. They can also be asked to facilitate team-building and trust-building experiences.

No matter how much groundwork you do, there are bound to be conflicts that arise. Conflict can, in fact, be a good sign as it usually occurs when people are truly engaged in what they are doing. Deal with conflicts immediately and with forthrightness and they'll be less likely to turn into feuds, grudges, or other ongoing problems.

As the Crow Flies

Fun is tricky business. Seriously. Even many famous comedians are known to be driven, focused, and serious when it comes to their work of making people laugh.

People have different ideas about how to have fun and you cannot please all the people all the time. But it's also true that watching others enjoy themselves generally makes people happy. So if you personally are having fun, then simply go with that feeling. Others may join you, smile from their position by the wall, or just roll their eyes in amusement.

Building trust within any community-wide effort takes time, patience, and creativity. Communities are unique, ever-changing organisms and thus the relationships and connections are dynamic and are influenced by many circumstances. Here are some suggestions for how to approach trust building:

► On a regular basis, change your leadership meeting venue. Invite but do not require (as it may not be comfortable or even possible) each participating member to host a gathering. Prior to getting down to business, ask your host to say a bit about the setting and perhaps lead a short tour.

► Publish a list of participants who are willing to share their names and detailed contact information. Some people will use this as a way to get to know names and a bit about others; some will use it to make personal connections.

► Begin each gathering of asset builders with an activity that emphasizes personal interaction. In most situations, these icebreakers or mixers work best if they are kept simple and brief, and if participants are encouraged to introduce themselves to people they don't know well or have never met before.

► Always have name tags and ask people to wear them. If appropriate, take time for check-ins and greetings.

► A good deal of the time people spend "listening" is used to plan the next thing they are going to say. Encourage asset builders to practice really listening to one another and see if it makes a difference in what they hear.

► Encourage asset builders to share information about the services and resources to which they have access. This can be done during regular meetings or on specific occasions. Emphasize that your efforts are focused on maximizing your community's positive influences on young people, not on replacing or changing what's currently available.

► Address personal differences and conflicts as soon as they arise. Focus on solutions rather than emotions and try to understand each party's perspective.

Questions to Consider

► What are you already doing to build trust among people in your community who are working on behalf of children and youth?

► What's the current level of trust among members of your initiative? Are there existing relationships that need attention or that can serve as starting points for trust building?

► What is the current level of trust between adults and youth in your community? Do you need to pay special attention to those relationships in order to be successful asset builders?

► What trust-building techniques have proven helpful in other forums?

► How can you go beyond paying lip service to the idea of building trust?

For More Information

In Good Company: Tools to Help Youth and Adults Talk (Search Institute, 2001).

As the Crow Flies

For some people, air travel defies logic. It makes little sense that a huge machine carrying lots of people can fly through the air for hundreds or thousands of miles and then land safely. It makes little sense, that is, unless you trust physics, the pilot, air traffic controllers, and so on. Most of us do trust air travel enough to do it. We trust because of our experiences and because of experiments we know others have done. But trust is fragile and easily broken. One bad landing and a lot of people are anxious about flying again for a long time. It's the same way with building trust in a community of asset builders. It accumulates, thanks to positive experiences and interactions. Betray someone's trust, though, and it takes a long time and a lot of work to gain it back.

Deal with Issues of Safety and Liability

We do not, thankfully, know of any true stories of an asset builder who has faced a situation in which a young person has come into harm's way as a result of the asset builder's actions. We also have no reports of adults who have been treated with suspicion or unfairly accused of misdeeds related to asset building. This is truly fortunate, but no reason to bury our heads in the sand. Accidents happen, mistakes are made, false accusations are lobbied, and children and youth are, tragically, sometimes preyed upon. Despite our best efforts, we cannot make this a perfect world for our young people. We can think ahead of time about how, within our initiatives, to prevent, disrupt, or—and we hope it never gets to this—deal with the consequences of such situations.

Safety and liability are large umbrellas that cover many topics. We've linked them here because the themes are similar: establishing and respecting appropriate boundaries, acting with honesty and integrity, keeping all parties safe, and so on. The themes tie strongly to some asset categories as well.

Helping Adults Move Safety out of Their *Comfort Zones*

One of the biggest issues when it comes to safety and liability is how willing adults are to move beyond their "comfort zones" and initiate new kinds of connections with young people. Men may have a particular challenge when it comes to building relationships with young people outside of their own families. Parent Educator Linda Silvius of Santa Clara County, California, says that while most parents she works with get excited about asset building, dads face different issues than moms. Because engaging with young people they don't know is a bigger risk for men (for fear of being perceived as threats rather than resources), many dads start doing more with young people in organized ways, such as coaching a team or getting to better know their kids' friends, according to Silvius.

When You Go

Some things are clear. An adult should never knowingly put a young person in a dangerous situation. Violence is unacceptable, as are romantic relationships between youth and adults. But there are many more conundrums than easy answers when it comes to safety and liability. Consider, for example:

▶ Are you, as an initiative, responsible in a legal and/or moral sense for the safety of those involved? If so, what are the potential consequences should something bad happen?

▶ Should you require background checks of all adults who want to be involved with your initiative? If so, who will facilitate the process? How will you pay for it?

▶ Is it okay for one adult to be alone with one young person? What if they are involved in a mentoring relationship? What if a young person needs a ride home from a meeting?

▶ Will you recommend that adults who are working with young people take out liability insurance policies in case something happens and a family decides to sue them?

▶ These are just a few of the questions. There are others that have to do with physical activity and injury, transportation, and so on.

But don't despair! Millions of people have decided that the risks are worth the benefit when it comes to building relationships with and supporting young people. There are things they do and that you can do, too, to prevent problems and to be poised to deal with them if they do occur.

The first, most basic step might be to establish a code of conduct to which all leadership members agree. The organizations that are represented by your group members may have documents that could be helpful in this process. Youth-serving organizations in particular have had to think about and deal with these issues. If you want to add some legal legitimacy to it you could consult an attorney who has experience in education, child care, youth work, or a related area. You could also convene a meeting of parents and talk with them about concerns they might have regarding asset building and "other adults" connecting with their children. You can also regularly check in with young people to find out if they have any concerns about how they are being treated.

Questions to Consider

▶ What are you currently doing to ensure the safety of your asset-building initiative participants?

▶ Will you require background checks of members of your initiative? Who will facilitate that? How will you pay for it?

▶ Do you want to investigate liability insurance for your initiative? If so, who can you turn to for information and advice?

▶ Are there safety or liability issues that are currently of concern to leadership group members? If so, what are they?

As the Crow Flies

In the foreword to *Connect 5: Finding the Caring Adults You May Not Realize Your Teen Needs* (Search Institute, 2004), Patty Wetterling, founder of the Jacob Wetterling Foundation, offers this reflection on safety in relationships between youth and adults:

When you think about it, one of the wonderful things about being a teen is the opportunity to meet new friends and expand your world. Over the years, since my son's kidnapping on October 22, 1989, I have learned about the sexual exploitation of children and the fear of abduction. The many other cases before and after Jacob have caused a troubling side effect of a general mistrust of any and everybody in the communities where a child has been victimized. Parents still tell their children "Don't talk to strangers," even though we know the victimization most often comes from someone the family of the child knows.

I profess that it is far better, as parents, to teach kids and especially teenagers how to talk to people so that they learn boundaries as well as what is and is not appropriate.

▶ Have you had to deal with safety or liability issues in the past? If so, how did it go? What were the outcomes?

For More Information

Guidelines for Screening of the Persons Working with Children, the Elderly, and Individuals with Disabilities in Need of Support (Office of Juvenile Justice and Delinquency Prevention, 1998).
Jacob Wetterling Foundation: www.jwf.org.

Work Through Roadblocks

Roadblocks can be defined simply as issues or situations that get in the way of progress. Less simple is figuring out how to deal with them. Though not always threatening, roadblocks are unsettling, regardless of how they arise. When people have caught the asset-building vision and are excited about what is happening, difficulties, resistance, and conflicts can be disheartening and frustrating. But an asset-building initiative is about change and innovation, and change and innovation usually create conflict and uncertainty.

Speed Bumps and Other Impediments

Sometimes teams face challenges early on, such as in Seattle where some human service organizations viewed the movement as a negative critique on their ability to provide services for families and young people in the community. And in Cape Elizabeth, Maine, there was a history of controversy and disagreement surrounding surveys of young people.

Other times problems come after the initiative is well in place. In Manchester, New Hampshire, as in other communities, the asset-building initiative got off to a decent start, but eventually ran into funding struggles that needed to be addressed.

Typical sources of difficulties are power struggles, mistrust, lack of leadership, disappointing results, or having a vague vision that is interpreted differently by different people. The issues you come up against will be unique to the climate and culture of your community.

When You Go

Few challenges are so great that they cannot be overcome. It's frustrating, certainly, when problems arise, but no reason to give up. In Seattle, for example, the initiative leaders worked with representatives of human service organizations to develop a five-page statement about asset building and human services having common goals and being mutually beneficial to the community. In Cape Elizabeth, the initiative leaders worked with young people to help them understand what would be done with the survey results, and with the media to lay the groundwork for the release of the data. The findings were discussed with youth first, giving them a chance to respond before it became public information. And in many communities facing funding issues, leaders have been creative, resourceful, and resilient.

The sense of being stuck when facing a seemingly insurmountable barrier is normal, and can lead to important discoveries about your group, your community, individuals, or other aspects of your asset-building efforts. If you can frame them this way, obstacles can become the impetus for reflection, examination, and renewed commitment.

So what can you do when you're stumped?

1. Ask for help. Check the Search Institute Web site at www.search-institute.org for ideas or referrals to other community initiatives. Or hire a consultant. Or seek out leaders of similar cross-sector efforts. Or ask some young people for their advice.
2. Seek to understand the context of the issue.
3. Make a list of what's going well and assess whether you can build on those strengths to help deal with your troubles.
4. Talk about it face to face. Avoiding conversation about problems usually leads to more problems. Being open and honest about the issues can build a network of people who can help deal with them.
5. Consider mediation, if appropriate. There are people trained in helping resolve disputes. If your obstacle involves a power struggle, dramatic difference of opinion, or other interpersonal conflict, it may be wise to bring in an expert consultant.
6. Keep in mind that this is a long-term effort. You don't have to overcome all obstacles right away. Some might just be around for a while. Given time, they may work themselves out or the answer may become clear.
7. Don't be afraid to decide that a parting of the ways or a change of course is what's needed.

Community Partners, a Massachusetts-based organization that promotes community development, has identified eight barriers—or roadblocks—that arise for community-wide initiatives. They are summarized on the worksheet "Working Through Roadblocks (on page 122). For each potential barrier, identify possible issues and solutions in your community.

Questions to Consider

▶ What are the obstacles you currently face?
▶ What causes the obstacles you face or have faced?
▶ What are you doing to address them?
▶ Are there obstacles you anticipate that you could potentially "head off"?

Get Media Attention and Coverage

There are many reasons to engage the media in your initiative. By doing so you ensure a wider potential audience for messages about asset building. You also tap into a pool of people who may be very interested in what they can do to support children and youth. In addition to caring about young people, members of the media may recognize (and you can help them see) that getting involved in asset building can lead to good stories and a positive public image for the station or publication.

Greater Than the Sum of the Parts

To spread the word about how much they value young people, the network television stations in Boise, Idaho, collaborated on a 13-week "Road Block" of public service announcements (PSAs) about Developmental Assets. Anyone watching any station during the selected times would see and hear the same asset-building message. The *Boise Family Magazine* and the *Idaho Statesman* newspaper also got involved by publishing asset-related articles.

Working Through Roadblocks

Roadblocks	Issues	Solutions
Turf and competition—Although your initiative is attempting to build coordination and cooperation, some organizations and groups will become competitive and territorial.		
Bad history—Previous initiatives in your community may not have done well and have given people the attitude that they've tried this before and it doesn't work.		
Failure to act—Too much planning can hurt an initiative. Have strategies in place for planning and action.		
Dominance by professionals—Initiatives should involve and empower residents, not just professionals and people in power.		
Poor links to the community—Meetings, planning, and action can become inaccessible to certain groups of your community.		
Minimal organizational capacity—Unclear vision, goals, objectives, and plans can hurt an initiative.		
Funding—Too much funding and too little funding can hurt an initiative. Community Partners found that initiatives started without funding and as grassroots groups often had more genuine community interest at the outset.		
Failure to provide and create leadership—An initiative has two leadership tasks: to provide competent leadership for the initiative and its tasks, and to create new leadership in the community.		
Costs outweigh the benefits—Busy people drop out when the costs (especially time) outweigh the benefits of being involved.		

When You Go

How can you include media people in your initiative? The first thing to do might be to invite one or more representatives to serve as part of your initiator or leadership group. If you don't have personal connections, you can start paying attention to which stations and publications run positive stories about young people or your community. The worksheet "Media Contact Information" (on page 125) can be used as a tool for systematically collecting this information. You may notice that one or two contacts seem to be particularly focused on issues that are also important to your group. It might make sense to start with them. Or you could request meetings with community service representatives from local outlets and ask them if there is anyone who might like to join you.

You can also strategically inform the media about events and happenings of your initiative. Learn how to prepare an effective press release, and only publicize events that you think are actually newsworthy. Be sure to include who is involved and invited, and what is happening. Include what need or interest is being met, and the time, date, and location of any event. Also note a contact person and phone number.

Here are some other ideas from *Get the Word Out: Communication Tools and Ideas for Asset Builders Everywhere* for effectively reaching the media:

► Create and regularly update a comprehensive media list. Employee newsletters, school papers or newsletters, congregational newsletters and bulletins, newsletters of civic and volunteer groups, and your city's newspaper and Web site are all potential vehicles for promoting your initiative. Editors of these smaller publications are often very accommodating. Also check with local radio programs, metro daily newspapers, and television news shows (including cable). Most of these have sections for community.

► Honor media deadlines. If you want to promote an upcoming event, you need to get the story in on time. To have a story featured on the evening television news it needs to happen early in the day or—if it's exceptionally newsworthy—at a time when it can be covered live.

► Pool your efforts and resources. Work with your local school district or city government to include asset-building information or a column in their newsletters, or arrange to have your own newsletter or flier mailed with theirs to save time and expenses.

► Feature children and youth in your events and media releases. The media want to run stories of young people; readers love them. Tell stories of adults working with young people or about teenagers engaged in asset-building activities.

► Ask local media to run regular asset-building features. Many newspapers and news shows have time or space set aside for "good news." Call the editors or producers and ask them to feature an "Asset a Day" or an "Asset Builder of the Week." The more specifics you offer, the better the chance they'll do it.

As the Crow Flies

Every once in a while, a roadblock that is ignored will eventually go away. We don't recommend this approach as a strategy to use very often, but it can be effective in cases where (a) the problem is with a person or group of persons who have very little power to impact what you're doing and who won't be easily convinced that it's a good idea, or (b) the issue isn't getting in your way and setting it aside for a while may change the circumstances surrounding it. There's the danger, of course, that letting things fester will simply make them worse, but if your network is strong and communication good you should be able to detect which way the train is going on the tracks.

▶ Send photos with media releases, but stay away from mug shots, "grip and grin" presentation photos, and group photos. Instead, show one or two people working together or a few people interacting. These shots have a much higher chance of being published and they more accurately communicate your message and mission. Make sure to include a note on the back of the photo that states who and what is pictured, and make sure to get photo releases (written permission) from everyone pictured.

▶ Create a news network for asset building in your community. You have to know what's going on to publicize it. The bigger the initiative, the harder that is to do. Ask teachers, young people, parents, and other community members to share their stories and successes with you or with media outlets.

▶ Select one person or small group of people to be in charge of publicity. This ensures that getting media coverage is always part of the planning and not just an afterthought.

Questions to Consider

▶ What, if any, types of media attention do you want? News? Public service announcements? Feature articles?

▶ What connections do you already have with members of the media?

▶ Do any members of your local media have histories of public service or focusing on community issues? If so, how do you reach out specifically to those people?

As the Crow Flies

Not all publicity is good publicity. You don't want the story to be that you've been working hard on something for three years and there is very little to show for it. So put yourselves in the driver's seat when it comes to getting the attention you want.

Go Further and Longer Than You Ever Thought You Could

Perhaps you're a couple of years into your asset-building initiative. You've experienced the first four phases of the change cycle—receptivity, awareness, mobilization, and action—in various manifestations. Now you're thinking about what's next. How do you keep it going? Where will you find new leaders to join you when others move on? What needs to be done to move into *continuity*, ensuring that the changes become a way of life for your community?

Or maybe you're just getting started and are wondering if an asset-building initiative is indeed a long-term viable option and not just another funding fad.

Good questions.

The National Asset-Building Case Study Project

While no one can say for sure what will happen in your community, we've been working with and learning from asset builders long enough to know that initiatives can be sustained over at least 10 years. They change, to be sure, but the thread of asset building appears to be strong enough to withstand the tugs and pulls.

To better understand how and why initiatives work or don't work, Search Institute undertook the National Asset-Building Case Study Project. Team members spent time immersed in four communities to study and learn about the changes they are making in support of the healthy development of children and youth. The four initiatives were the Moorhead Healthy Community Initiative in Moorhead, Minnesota, started in 1994; the Take the Time Initiative in Multnomah County, Portland, Oregon, launched in 1997; the GivEm40 24.7 Coalition in the Traverse Bay Area of Michigan, started in 1999; and the Healthy Community Initiative of Greater Orlando, Florida, in existence since 1998.

Some of what you'll find in this section is gleaned from the findings of that study. Other elements are drawn from the wisdom and experience of other researchers, community members, trainers, and leaders who were all readily willing to share what they know, believe, and hope for.

Media Contact Information

Organization: _____

Primary contact (name, title): _____

Other contacts (names, titles): _____

Address: _____

City, State, ZIP: _____

Phone: _____

Fax: _____

E-mail: _____

Type of media:
- ☐ Network television
- ☐ Cable television
- ☐ Internet
- ☐ Newspaper
- ☐ Newsletter
- ☐ Magazine
- ☐ Radio
- ☐ Other:

_____

_____

Frequency:
- ☐ Daily
- ☐ Weekly
- ☐ Monthly
- ☐ Bimonthly
- ☐ Quarterly
- ☐ Other:

_____

_____

Audience demographics (geographic reach, population): _____

Deadline: _____

Special issues or segments: _____

Areas of particular interest: _____

Previous stories about this initiative: _____

Last updated: _____

When You Go

Based on experiences, case studies, and insights of asset builders across North America, here are eight tips for sustaining your initiative:

1. *Approach community change as a dynamic process.* Be willing to go with the flow as long as the focus remains on your vision and mission.
2. *Give it away.* Asset building is not a program or a process, it's a way of life. Rejoice when people take steps at their own pace in their own time.
3. *Combine planning and doing.* Be intentional about your action, and keep moving forward.
4. *Make sure to renew and broaden leadership.*
5. *Always remember that money is not the central focus.* Money is one form of energy; you need lots of other types as well.
6. *Build relationships.* Relationships are what asset building is all about.
7. *Include evaluation.* Know that good evaluation is rooted in good planning, which is rooted in good evaluation.
8. *Trust the community.*

Asset-building initiatives unfold in nonlinear and unpredictable ways. As initiatives evolve across time they go through periods of clarity, stability, and regularity. These are points at which funding is secure, staffing and key major players are consistent, and progress is being made on community building, social movement, and community infrastructure.

There are also periods of instability, where things become difficult and challenging. During these times, partnerships begin to feel unstable and the future looks less certain; also, funding can become precarious, people who have been involved and influential may move on or changes roles, roadblocks are more noticeable, and it's harder to see whether you're making a difference.

The periods of stability are opportunities to move forward with purpose and garner accomplishments. The periods of uncertainly can, surprisingly, become opportunities for highly positive change. In some ways these difficult times are like coming to the intersection of a number of roads. With signs pointing every which way, there can be a lot of stress and confusion. But these "crises" mark moments of opportunity to reconfirm shared commitments, reconfigure the caravan, and move forward down an even better path.

Questions to Consider

► How has your initiative been successful so far? What can you do to celebrate and build on those successes?

► What things are not working so well? How can you best address those areas of concern?

► Are you where you thought you'd be at this point? If not, why not? Is where you are okay? Or are there people who are frustrated or dismayed about your progress or lack thereof? What are the implications of these dynamics?

► What resources would help you deepen your efforts and sustain them over the long haul? How accessible are they? What do you need to do to access them?

For More Information

Consider attending the annual Healthy Communities • Healthy Youth Conference held in various locations across the United States. Information is available online at www.search-institute.org.

As the Crow Flies

The asset-building movement is, in many ways, in its preadolescence. We have yet to see what a fully mature initiative looks like. We do know, however, that those showing the most promise have profound long-range visions, coupled with realistic expectations about what they can accomplish in shorter-term increments.

Chapter 4

Documenting the Journey

This section looks at how to understand, learn from, and record your community's asset-building experiences.

Don't Miss It
▶ Make Sense of Reflection and Evaluation
▶ Build an Evaluation Team
▶ Identify and Answer Key Questions
▶ Communicate the Results of Evaluation

Make Sense of Reflection and Evaluation

For some initiatives, reflection is simply a time to celebrate successes and to informally revise strategies that are not working as well. For others, evaluation stands out as something entirely separate from planning, implementation, and reflection; evaluation is about numbers and documentation and paperwork.

Funders may require that organizations defend what they do and make the case that it's worth continuing. But those attitudes are changing as more foundations, civic leaders, and other supporters embrace the Developmental Assets framework and the idea of focusing on strengths. Just as communities are undertaking long-term efforts, many grant makers are changing the way they allocate funds.

At its best, evaluation is a collaborative learning process that can help you identify methods for improving your mobilization and asset-building efforts and reporting on what has resulted from them. This is sometimes known as *participatory evaluation.* Author and evaluator Michael Patton describes the process like this:

> One of the negative connotations often associated with evaluation is that it is something done to people. One is evaluated. Participatory evaluation, in contrast, is a process controlled by the people in the program or community. It is something they undertake as a formal, reflective process for their own development and empowerment *Qualitative Evaluation Methods*, 2nd ed., (Thousand Oaks, CA: Sage Publications, 1990).

Regardless of your financially driven evaluation needs, you can and should build into your efforts reflection and evaluation that will give you the information you need to help strengthen your initiative.

An Asset-Building EKG for HEART of OKC

Through an extensive review of its efforts, Healthy, Empowered And Responsible Teens of Oklahoma City (HEART of OKC) is one of the first initiatives to generate some of the best, most up-to-date scientific evidence of the effectiveness of a positive approach to youth development. The evaluation is unique for several reasons. We share the story not as a process to emulate, but because it includes some real-life examples of creative approaches to understanding where you've been, where you are, and where you're headed.

The initiative began in 1995 as one of 13 adolescent pregnancy prevention initiatives funded by the Centers for Disease Control (CDC). The project team, led by coordinator Sharon Rodine, insisted on beginning its efforts with a holistic approach at the neighborhood level. Believing that the most effective strategies combine prevention, health promotion, and positive youth development, HEART of OKC established a list of goals that included preventing pregnancy, as well as reducing related risk-taking behaviors (such as violence or alcohol and other drug use) and promoting protective factors (assets). "We start with the young person," says Rodine, "not with a disease or body part."

For the first two years of the grant, the project team members spent much of their time and other resources learning about the community's deficits and strengths through an extensive needs-and-assets assessment. In collaboration with researchers and evaluators from the University of Oklahoma, HEART of OKC staff members gathered demographic data, surveyed teens and their parents, held focus groups and interviews, and conducted *windshield tours.* Adds Rodine:

> We got in our cars and drove around, looking through our windshields, documenting what we saw. We took pictures, wrote notes, looked at what was there and what was not . . . anything to give a visual sense of the community. We were like detectives, out there gathering information from the community.

With this foundation of information, the team identified best practices and began helping people in the community make important connections to better serve young people. Rodine describes this work as "matching resources with resources." At the same time, independent researchers and evaluators gathered the scientific evidence that CDC requires of grantees. To better understand the relationships between assets, risk behaviors, and neighborhood factors, these scientists developed a survey used to obtain data from more than 1,300 pairs of teens and parents.

The findings from their survey show positive impacts on a number of health-related behaviors among Oklahoma youth, and have shed significant light on how assets work. The researchers have written a number of scientific articles for a variety of journals.

When You Go

What are you trying to do? How are you going about doing it? How do you know you're making a difference? What has actually happened or been changed by your efforts? What kinds of data can you provide to show that your efforts are effective and to guide future decisions and strategies?

You may be asking these questions of yourselves. Or perhaps parents, youth, policy makers, educators, funders, and community members want to know. Whoever is asking deserves answers so that you and they can determine where your efforts are succeeding and where you can improve.

Here are descriptions of the three basic types of evaluation, each of which was used in the Oklahoma evaluation:

Developmental or *process evaluation* focuses on continuous improvement and adaptation. The data gathered help refine the effort.

Implementation evaluation emphasizes assessing the degree to which major components of the effort are progressing as planned, finding explanations for successes and failures, and assessing impact based on a pre-determined set of indicators.

Outcome evaluation assesses the effects of the effort on stakeholders (e.g., young people, asset champions, schools, community organizations).

You do not necessarily need to hire an evaluator. Developmental/process and implementation evaluations are often best designed and conducted within an initiative, sometimes with the help of a consultant. Outcome evaluations are more complex and complicated, and unless you have an experienced evaluator on your team, they are best conducted by an outside expert.

Most initiatives won't have the interest or capacity to undertake an evaluation of the magnitude of the one done by HEART of OKC. There are, however, a number of simple tools you can use that can provide helpful and important information about what's going well with your initiative and your young people, and what things may need extra work. There are four key steps to conducting an evaluation:

1. Building an evaluation team;
2. Establishing goals (see page 134);
3. Identifying and answering key questions; and
4. Interpreting and reporting the findings.

The next several sections provide information to help you take each step, as well as ideas and issues to consider as you move through the process.

Working with External Evaluators

Rebecca N. Saito, author of *What's Working? Tools for Evaluating Your Mentoring Program* (Search Institute, 2001), suggests using these filters when hiring a professional evaluator. Choose someone who:

- Understands and is committed to asset building and/or community change;
- Is concerned with meeting your needs and ensuring that the evaluation is useful to you;
- Is comfortable balancing scientific rigor, practicality, and utility;
- Will be able to effectively communicate and interpret findings to help you not only relate your initiative's successes, but also improve its effectiveness; and
- Is good at both planning or conceptualizing and conducting an evaluation that will meet your needs within your time and budget constraints.

If you need ideas for possible candidates, consider asking:
- Other initiatives in your state or region;
- Youth- or family-serving program providers in your area;
- Your local higher-education institute or 4-H office; or
- Your local United Way.

Questions to Consider

► Are there people involved with your initiative who have experience with evaluation? How can you tap their expertise?

► Has your group conducted evaluations in the past? What were the successes and challenges of those experiences?

► Are you considering hiring a professional evaluator? If so, what criteria will you use to select the person?

For More Information

Visit Search Institute's Web page for details about other evaluation products and services: www.search-institute.org/research/eval.html.

Build an Evaluation Team

Perhaps the real first step in evaluation is to approach the task with an attitude of caring and a focus on improvement. Novelist John Updike once said, "Any activity becomes creative when the doer cares about doing it right, or doing it better." And, as we've pointed out already, that's what reflection and evaluation are all about. To help you maintain this attitude and focus, we recommend that you design and conduct your evaluation by working with a team

As the Crow Flies

A surprising roadblock to effective evaluation is language. The intended meanings of terms such as *outcomes, objectives, assessment,* and *process* are often lost in translation. Spend time at the beginning on clarifying terms and, if necessary, creating written definitions to distribute to team members as reminders. If you are not completing a formal evaluation process to meet funding requirements, you may have better luck talking about "reflection" and "improvement" instead.

who can support and help you in your effort. This team should include young people, and they should have an equal voice to adults.

Listening to Youth Voices

Justin Macy understands the difference between just being involved and truly having an equal voice. Macy is a young veteran of youth groups, youth empowerment programs, and youth leadership training. He says he's seen enough to know that even when the "higher ups" say a program is engaging young people, the reality is often a much different truth.

There was something unique, though, that he saw in Youth as Evaluators, a joint venture between the University of Wisconsin at Madison and Cornell University in Ithaca, New York. "I've been in youth groups my entire life," says Macy (who reports that he has 27 of the 40 Developmental Assets).

> I realized that with a tool like this, I could point out that the youth voice isn't out there as much as everyone thinks it is . . . a youth voice is always going to be a little more unrealistic and more creative than an adult voice, and an adult voice will be a little more rational and a little less risk taking. But when they work together, the adults will keep the youth on the ground and let the youth do a number of things they would otherwise not be able to do.

Buffy Peterson is the adult advisor for the Youth as Evaluators project. She's also the coordinator of the Jefferson County, New York, chapter of Assets Coming Together for Youth (ACT), a pilot site for Youth as Evaluators. She explains that four adults and four youth are working together on the following objectives:

► To develop a set of research tools that measure the scope and quality of "youth voice,"—in other words, the extent to which young people are meaningfully involved in decision making, planning, and the sharing of power with adults within community and organizational contexts.

► To develop an innovative evaluation methodology, where youth-adult partnerships are formed, for collecting and using data to bring about organizational change and improvement.

▶ To evaluate the utility of the tools and approach for assessing and fostering youth voice within organizations and communities, and measuring progress toward attainment of youth development goals.

▶ To partner with youth in all aspects of the evaluation—from designing the tools, developing and implementing the evaluation approach, and analyzing the findings, to disseminating the results.

One result of the team's collaboration was the Youth Empowerment Tool, a set of surveys—one for youth, one for adults—that takes about 10 minutes to complete and provides a picture of the true nature of youth engagement within a program. The Youth as Evaluators team analyzes the data and presents them back to the program. The point is not, Macy says, "to criticize," but to offer ideas and suggestions for improvement.

When You Go

Assets Coming Together for Youth is not alone in the effort to engage youth in evaluation. It is a growing trend among strengths-based supporters of child and youth development. UNICEF has created a guide on the topic. And the Spring 2003 issue of the *Community Youth Development* journal focused on youth engagement in evaluation. Editors Leslie Goodyear and Barry Checkaway write:

> Programs that involve young people in research and evaluation projects benefit from youths' 'local knowledge' as they collaborate with adults to plan, implement, and report findings of evaluations. Evaluators have the chance to actively engage and educate a new generation of community members, effectively socializing future stakeholders to the importance of evaluation for democratic decision making in programs and communities.

The Harvard Family Research Project in Cambridge, Massachusetts, has also studied youth involvement in evaluation and offers these elements that aid success (from Issues and Opportunities in Out-of-School Time Evaluation Briefs, *Youth Involvement in Evaluation & Research,* No. 1, February 2002):

1. Organizational and community readiness;
2. Adequate training and support for involved youth;
3. Adequate training and support for adult staff;
4. Selecting the right team; and
5. Sustaining youth involvement.

In addition to fully engaging young people, seek representation from the organizations and groups that are most interested in the results of your evaluation. Finally, also involve funders or at least review your evaluation plans with them so that any concerns can surface and be resolved.

The worksheet "Our Evaluation Team" (on page 132) will help you identify potential team members, facilitate your team members' coming to a shared understanding of what they see as evaluation, and help your team monitor and improve your evaluation efforts.

Questions to Consider

▶ Who should be part of the evaluation team? What role will each person play? What roles do current team members see themselves playing?

▶ When team members hear the word *evaluation,* what comes to mind? Why?

▶ What are the differences and similarities in how team members think of evaluation?

Identify and Answer Key Questions

Good evaluation questions can help you design and structure your overall evaluation effort. The key is to prioritize what you need to learn and then choose your questions accordingly.

If you are doing an evaluation within your initiative rather than hiring a consultant, we recommend focusing on no more than three to five questions. They generally take time to develop, so don't try to rush the process. Also remember that by engaging young people, you bring an element to evaluation that will be different and perhaps unsettling to many people.

Our Evaluation Team

Use this worksheet to identify which people should be part of your evaluation team.

Name, telephone number, and e-mail address	Perspective(s) he or she brings and/or organizations he or she represents (youth, youth-serving experience or organizations, adults, funders, business, congregations, school, etc.)	Previous evaluation skills or experience (circle one)
		Yes/No
		Yes/No
		Yes/No
		Yes/No
		Yes/No
		Yes/No
		Yes/No

Different Perspectives Lead to Different Questions

Young people often have different questions and ideas about what's important to know. Pat Seppanen, formerly with the University of Minnesota and now director of Research Applications at Search Institute, offers as an example a story about *New Moon: The Magazine for Girls and Their Dreams*. *New Moon*, based in Duluth, Minnesota, is a girl-run publication. With funding from the Kellogg Foundation the editorial board was able to attend the World Conference for Women in Beijing in 2001. Part of the grant stipulated that they needed to develop a platform for girls, because while similar issues impact girls and women, there are clearly differences. Seppanen was hired to evaluate their efforts.

Letting the girls take the lead, she discovered their interests were far from preparing a survey about the booklet they developed that outlined their platform. Instead, they wanted people's real reactions: how they felt, what they experienced. So they handed out copies to women at the conference and then talked to them. They also wrote postcards describing their experiences that were published in a Minnesota newspaper. In short, the evaluation was focused on personal reactions and reflections, and the process was fluid, experiential, and far from the outcome-focused efforts that many adults are used to.

When You Go

To begin identifying your questions, decide whether you want to focus on process, implementation, or outcomes. If your focus is on outcomes, make sure you review the goals you have identified. If your focus is on process or implementation, make sure you review the steps you plan to take to achieve your goals. Then, using simple, concrete, and unambiguous language, draft your set of questions.

Consult at this point (or prior to developing the questions) with the stakeholders who are most interested in your evaluation and your findings. Ask whether the questions seem like the right ones, and whether the answers will lead to the data they want or need. You can then refine and sharpen the focus on your questions by clarifying how you are going to answer and report on them.

Moving Toward Answers

While the use of surveys or questionnaires is perhaps the most common way to gather data, evaluation can be much more. Choosing methods is another place where wise communities listen to and learn from young people. The most important role of adults on your evaluation team may be to teach young people what they need to know, coach them in how to refine and implement their ideas, and then learn together from the experience as well as the information.

Using a Logic Model

Lawrence Pasti, director of the Integrated County Planning project (ICP) in New York, has developed one simple formula for measuring outcomes. This type of tool is known as a *logic model*. See the worksheet "Creating a Logic Model" (on page 134). It is often used in evaluation planning and is a good place to start identifying and answering the questions you have.

Pasti also suggests using the following questions to help you determine the best evaluation methods to use, based on the logic model you've created.

► What are the desired outcomes of this intervention?
► What type of measure or evidence do you have of this outcome?

As the Crow Flies

Beware of building an evaluation team whose members are too invested in the initiative to be objective about the process and outcomes. This may be particularly relevant in smaller communities or initiatives where "everybody does everything." If the people involved aren't able to step back and examine the true picture of what's happening related to asset building, you'll end up with information that will not be truly useful in strengthening your efforts.

Creating a Logic Model

As you assess your needs and your desired outcomes, remember to focus on existing strengths and accomplishments. Concentrating on deficits can be limiting.

Needs (The needs/conditions that must be addressed . . .)	
Goals (We hope to achieve . . .)	
Interventions (By doing the following . . .)	
Short-term Outcomes (We expect the following changes to occur . . .)	
Long-term Outcomes (We will know we are reaching our goals if . . .)	

➤ What methods will be used to measure the outcome? (Indicate methods for collecting data such as surveys, questionnaires, or observations.)

➤ When will the data be collected? (Provide an estimate of the month and year.)

➤ Who will be responsible for making sure the data are collected? (Give the name of at least one person.)

➤ What evaluation design will be used? (Indicate designs such as pre/post, post only, or follow-up.)

Please note that these questions are complex. If you do conduct such an in-depth evaluation, you may benefit from the expertise of a professional evaluator. If you conduct an evaluation based on a logic model, try using the worksheet "Measuring Outcomes" (on page 136) to help plan your data collection.

A Variety of Approaches

Keeping track of facts (e.g., number and type of events, participation levels, awareness raising efforts, media coverage, and so on) is another way to document your initiative's story. Generally, combining this tactic and other methods works best to give you the breadth and depth of information that you need. Consider these possibilities:

One-on-one interviews in person or by telephone—This method often is based on a written questionnaire, but the questions and responses are spoken. Advantages include quick responses, potentially getting responses from more people, and making personal contacts with community members.

On the other hand, it's time intensive to make the calls, and anonymity is lost so the responses may not be as honest as with a written survey.

Focus groups—Information from focus groups can be richer than what you get through a written survey. People express their feelings and thoughts in ways that are impossible to capture on paper. You also have opportunities to follow up in areas that seem vague or unclear.

On the other hand, unless focus groups are skillfully designed and led, the results may not be accurate or helpful. Many groups will need to be guided to stay on a topic. Focus groups are best led by someone with prior experience.

Current records and observations— This type of data provides limited and/or anecdotal information and is best used as a supplement.

Others—Other possible strategies include photo journaling, video documentation, voice recordings, and story mapping. For example, I. Shelby Andress and the asset-building initiative in northern Nevada developed a grid to see where they were in terms of the phases of change within each of the five action strategies. They indicated where they thought each asset-building organization in the community was on the change pathway. They were surprised, says Andress, to find that most of the transformation had been up through mobilization, with little in the areas of action and continuity. The findings helped them plan their next steps in light of their past successes and challenges. To discuss your own progress in these areas, use the worksheet "Moving along the Change Pathway" (on page 137).

Sometimes a more general survey is all you need to gather feedback from the people in your community. If so, try using the "Background Information Form" (on page 138), "Initial Assessment of an Asset-Building Initiative" (on page 139), and "Healthy Community Rating Sheet" (on page 140) or incorporate the content into your own lists of survey questions.

As the Crow Flies

Many people enjoy thinking about all the positive things that can be learned through evaluation. For this reason it's important to have someone in the role of devil's advocate or gatekeeper when it comes to choosing your questions. Some groups have one or more people who naturally ask critical questions, but if you do not have such a person in your initiative it's wise to "appoint" someone. This can help you avoid the temptation of selectively considering only the desirable information you gather instead of looking at what the data actually show.

Measuring Outcomes

When conducting an evaluation based on a logic model, you may find this chart helpful in planning your data collection.

Outcome	Measure/Indicator	Method	Collection Date	Person Responsible	Evaluation Design

Moving along the Change Pathway

Consider each of the five action strategies listed in the column on the left, and assess the progress you've made so far. Which individuals, groups, and organizations are becoming open to or aware of your goals? Which are actively helping you achieve positive change?

	Receptivity: Being open to change	Awareness: Understanding the possibilities of change	Mobilization: Organizing for change	Action: Making change happen	Continuity: Ensuring that the changes become a way of life
Engage Adults Mobilize adults from all walks of life to develop sustained, strength-building relationships with children and adolescents, both within families and in neighborhoods.					
Mobilize Young People Activate young people to use their power as asset builders and change agents.					
Activate Sectors Transform all sectors—such as families, neighborhoods, schools, congregations, businesses, youth organizations, human services, and health care organizations—to create an asset-building culture and to contribute fully to young people's healthy development.					
Invigorate Programs Invigorate, expand, and enhance asset-rich programs to become more asset-rich and to be available to and accessed by all children and youth.					
Influence Civic Decisions Influence decision makers and opinion leaders to leverage financial, media, and policy resources in support of this positive transformation of communities and society.					

Background Information Form

Date:_____

Please answer these background questions before you begin the questionnaire that follows.

a. How old are you? (circle one)
   13–19
   20–29
   30–49
   50–64
   65 or older

b. Are you female or male? (circle one)   Male   Female

c. Are you (please circle the one that indicates your main occupation):
   A full-time student
   A full-time paid worker
   A full-time homemaker
   Other:_____

d. How are you involved in the group or organization that has asked you to fill out the following question-
   naire? (circle all that apply)
   Student
   Parent or guardian
   Participant
   Leader
   Volunteer
   Interested resident
   Neighbor

e. What race or ethnic term is most accurate for you? (circle one)
   African American/Black
   Asian American
   Caucasian/Anglo/White
   Hispanic/Latino/Latina
   Native American/American Indian/Eskimo
   Multiracial
   Other:_____

Initial Assessment of an Asset-Building Initiative

1. What do participants in this effort consider to be most promising?

2. What keeps people involved in this effort?

3. What are the most significant barriers or challenges to this effort?

4. What should be done about these barriers or challenges?

Healthy Community Rating Sheet

For each of the characteristics listed here, decide whether you strongly agree (SA), agree (A), disagree (D), or strongly disagree (SD) with each statement and circle the corresponding letter(s). If you don't know, mark an X in the margin next to that characteristic and think about how you can find out.

Engage Adults

1. Most adults take personal responsibility for the well-being of the community's children and youth.

   SA   A   D   SD

2. Most adults make time to build Developmental Assets for and with all children and youth who come into their spheres of influence.

   SA   A   D   SD

3. Most adults respect and value young people for who they are and for who they are becoming.

   SA   A   D   SD

4. Most adults learn and practice trustworthiness and relationship-building skills.

   SA   A   D   SD

5. Adults take steps to increase their involvement in organizational and community actions on behalf of young people.

   SA   A   D   SD

Mobilize Youth

6. Most young people take personal responsibility for their own well-being and that of their peers.

   SA   A   D   SD

7. Most young people build their own assets as well as those of their peers.

   SA   A   D   SD

8. Most young people feel valued and valuable in the community.

   SA   A   D   SD

9. Most young people have significant, positive relationships with adults.

   SA   A   D   SD

10. Most young people are actively involved in the community.

    SA   A   D   SD

Invigorate Programs

11. Most organizations throughout the community mobilize their internal asset-building capacities to create asset-promoting policies, systems, and structures.

    SA   A   D   SD

12. Most organizations make assistance and support readily available to everyone in the community.

    SA   A   D   SD

13. Most organizations train workers and administrators in the asset framework and in asset-building strategies.

    SA   A   D   SD

Activate Sectors

14. Developmental needs and assets of youth are a regular topic of conversation in congregations, schools, health care, business, and other socializing sectors within the community.

    SA   A   D   SD

15. Most neighborhoods are places of caring.

    SA   A   D   SD

16. Most neighborhoods are places of support.

    SA   A   D   SD

17. Most neighborhoods are places of safety.

    SA   A   D   SD

Influence Civic Decisions

18. The community incorporates shared values, boundaries, and expectations regarding youth in its sense of identity.

    SA   A   D   SD

19. Developmental needs and assets of youth are a regular topic of conversation throughout the community and are articulated as a community priority.

    SA   A   D   SD

20. Youth needs and challenges in the community are recognized and addressed from a positive youth development perspective.

    SA   A   D   SD

21. Youth are a visible, active, and positive force in community life.

    SA   A   D   SD

Conducting Focus Groups

The following information can help you decide whether or not, and how, to conduct focus groups or other open-ended methods of questioning. It is advice adapted from *Focus Groups: A Practical Guide for Applied Research* by Richard Krueger and Mary Anne Casey (3rd ed., 2000).

1. *Choose the right questions.* Be clear about how the responses from each question will help you answer your overall evaluation questions. Use your time wisely by including only those questions that are essential.
2. *Consider your audience.* Picture the range of participants, imagine how they might interpret each question, and word questions accordingly.
3. *Use open-ended questions* that allow participants to create their own responses rather than having to choose from a specified list of answers. Avoid questions that can be answered with a yes or no.
4. *Be careful about asking why*—it can make people feel defensive. Instead, consider asking "What was it about . . . ?" Or, "What prompted . . . ?" Or, "What features of . . . did you like?"
5. *Use "think back" questions.* It's easier for people, especially young people, to think back to an experience than to project or imagine forward.
6. *Consider the order of your questions.* Your first questions should be easy and comfortable. It is sometimes best to start with a simple question or introductions and go around the group, having everyone answer it (this is called a *round robin*). Sequence your questions from general to specific.
7. *Avoid asking leading questions* that direct or inhibit responses. For instance, do not say, "I'm sure there were many problems you encountered in your first year as an initiative. What were some of them?" Rather, ask something like "Were there any challenging or difficult times during your first year as an initiative? If so, would you describe some of them for me?"
8. *Be careful when asking questions where social desirability is strong*—that is, where an answer is perceived to be "right" or "preferred." Reassure participants that you want them to be as honest and open as they can be to make the evaluation most useful.
9. *Give your questions a trial run.* Use the questions as the basis for an interview with an individual or group of people who resemble (or share similar experiences with) the participants whom you will invite to the focus group. Make sure the questions you have designed elicit responses that give you the information you need to answer your evaluation questions. Reword any questions that did not draw out helpful information or were difficult for respondents to answer.

Questions to Consider

➤ What do you want to know about your community or your initiative?
➤ Why do you want to know this?
➤ How will you use what you learn?
➤ What do you need to do to link your key questions to your goals and anticipated outcomes?

For More Information

Developing Questions for Focus Groups (Thousand Oaks, CA: Sage Publications, 1998).

Communicate the Results of Evaluation

One of the most important factors to consider when preparing to present information from an evaluation is how the people who are asking the key questions *prefer to learn.* If the word *evaluation* conjures up images of thick studies or reports, it's time to reshape people's thinking a bit. It may be appropriate to use formal research language when addressing a funder or government organization, but you may want to use more conversational terms when addressing groups of community members.

Going Beyond the Numbers

John McKnight, co-creator of Asset-Based Community Development (ABCD), once wrote:

> In universities, people know through studies. In businesses and bureaucracies, people know by reports. In communities, people know by . . . community stories [that] allow people to reach back into their common history and their individual experience for knowledge about truth and direction for the future.

He further stated that there is a danger in trying to quantify community change work because quantitative (numbers-based) evaluation "is a tongue that ignores their own capacities and insights."

When You Go

As you explore how to share your findings, it may be helpful to think of it as "telling your initiative's story." Then really encourage your team to think outside the evaluation box.

As an example of the kinds of innovative approaches being used, Pat Seppanen describes a conference session she attended a number of years ago. The presenters had been hired to evaluate a college's effort to become more welcoming to students of color. They interviewed students, faculty, and staff. But instead of putting the findings into a report, the team developed a sort of theatrical presentation. "Actors" would come on stage and read quotes from the conversations. The mediums for gathering and sharing the findings were powerful and appropriate, says Seppanen, because "race and ethnicity are so much about self. Survey data doesn't personalize it the way this did."

You'll probably find that your presentation will vary depending on your audience and the medium (e.g., report, article, presentation). Some groups will appreciate a PowerPoint presentation followed by small group discussions, and others may prefer simple but inspirational storytelling. Whatever method you choose, the worksheets "What We're Learning" (on page 143) and "Evaluation Findings Summary" (on page 144) can help you filter through and organize the information in useful, practical ways.

Questions to Consider

► Who are the key groups to which you need to report your findings?
► How are you going to report to each group?
► Do you need someone to check your reports for accuracy? If so, who could do this?

For More Information

Getting to Outcomes 2004: Promoting Accountability Through Methods for Planning, Implementation, and Evaluation (Santa Monica, CA: RAND Corporation, 2004).

As the Crow Flies

Your evaluation needs will likely depend largely on your sources of income and other support. If you receive grants, particularly government grants, there will be specific guidelines you must follow when reporting on your efforts. We cannot stress enough the importance of taking evaluation seriously as part of your plan rather than something that comes at the "end" or at certain milestones. Making the most of evaluation requires thoughtful, intentional integration into your overall asset-building efforts.

What We're Learning

Our key questions:

Tools and processes we've used to answer them:

Key learnings or knowledge gained:

Surprises or puzzles:

Evaluation Findings Summary

Initiative or Organization name:

Date:

Evaluation question:

This question is particularly relevant to (specify goal):

Action steps taken toward this goal:

Tools used to gather data:

Key findings:

Other relevant data or information:

Outside factors that affected data gathering and may affect findings:

Remaining data to be gathered:

Epilogue

The world lost a remarkable asset builder just as this resource was beginning to take shape. After living with cancer for seven years (despite an original six-month prognosis) Search Institute's Director of National Initiatives, Laura Lee Geraghty, passed away in January 2004.

Laura Lee had at an early age committed her life to making a difference in the world. She worked in volunteerism and community service before joining Search Institute in 1998. She said that though some of her colleagues questioned the change, she saw asset building as a continuation of a career-long commitment to "helping people take control where they can and exercise their responsibilities."

"Taking responsibility is ultimately the bedrock of responsibility," she reflected. And, true to form, as the founding director of the Search Institute's national Healthy Communities • Healthy Youth initiative, she helped asset builders from Alaska to Florida to Canada to Australia take personal and collective responsibility for their young.

I sat with Laura Lee in her home shortly before she died. The reason for my visit was to talk about her ideas for this guide and, in particular, whether she would be willing to write a preface. We had worked together for eight years, but never taken the time to just sit and talk. There was always too much to do, not enough time, and so on.

So we ended up on that sunny November day relaxing together for the first and last time. We talked about family, friends, and our work. She asked—as was her inclination—important, critical, and influential questions about this project: Whose voices do we want to reflect? What difference will this make in the world? Is there information that we need to share with others engaged in this work that can best be conveyed in this format?

As a person who struggles with the meaning of difficult life transitions, I was struck by the grace, humor, dignity, confidence, and passion for this work that she embodied, even as her body failed her.

We came to agree on two things: it was indeed important for me to revise the approach of this resource; and I would draft a "ghost-written" preface for her to revise and edit. The latter we decided because she wasn't convinced she would have the stamina to write one herself. The former we concluded because, as she said, "though we still believe that every community needs to do this themselves, there are things that we have learned are successful and we ought to more boldly say that."

She expressed hope that *The Journey of Community Change* would help more people more effectively share with the others the vision of asset-rich environments for young people. Talking about her young grandson and her dream that every child in the world would have the loving, supportive environment he takes for granted, she noted, "He just thinks it's the way the world is." She reminisced about friends who have given up work to care for their grandchildren, or adjusted their living situations to help their families, calling these actions "gifts those kids will hold forever."

Through our hours together Laura Lee easily moved from talking about national and global change to speaking of personal transformation. She reflected on asset-building stories she'd seen recently in the media, and how she hoped the framework would continue to provide people with the language to describe what we want for everyone's children, particularly for youth. "Little kids evoke emotions," she said. "Teenagers are harder to get to and it's harder to describe where we want to be with them."

Laura Lee wasn't able to review the draft preface I sent to her and thus I cannot in good conscience publish it. Instead I offer my reflections on my glimpse into the character of this true asset champion, in the hope that knowing how she navigated the paths she took in her life will inspire you as you journey toward a community-wide initiative that reaches far and wide, deep and high.